Developing the Leader
Within You *Workbook*

Developing the Leader Within You *Workbook*

JOHN C. MAXWELL

THOMAS NELSON
Since 1798

NASHVILLE   DALLAS   MEXICO CITY   RIO DE JANEIRO   BEIJING

Published in Nashville, Tennessee, by Thomas Nelson, Inc.

Scripture quotations are fron the NEW KING JAMES VERSION of the Bible. Copyright © 1979, 1980, 1982, Thomas Nelson, Inc., Publishers.

ISBN 0-7852-6725-5
ISBN 978-0-7852-6725-6
Printed in the United States of America
28 29 VG 11

Table of Contents

Introduction

THE LEADER WITHIN YOU

It was a moment I will never forget. I was lecturing on the subject of leadership and we had just taken a fifteen-minute break. A man named Bob rushed up to me and said, "You have saved my career! Thank you so much." As he turned to walk away, I stopped him and asked, "How have I 'saved' your career?" He replied, "I'm fifty-three years old and for the last seventeen years I have been in a position that demands leadership. Up until recently I have struggled, acutely aware of my lack of leadership skills and success. Last year I attended your leadership seminar and learned principles that I immediately began applying in my work situation. And it happened. People began to follow my direction—slowly at first, but now quite readily. I had plenty of experience, but no expertise. Thanks for making me a leader!"

Testimonials like Bob's have encouraged me to devote much of my time to developing leaders. It is the reason why I hold leadership seminars in the United States and other countries. It is the reason for this workbook and my other resources.

What you are about to work through is a culmination of skills learned in more than two decades of leading people. For many years I have taught these leadership principles and watched with great satisfaction as men and women have become more effective in leading others. Now I have the opportunity to share them with you.

LEADERSHIP CAN BE TAUGHT

Leadership is not an exclusive club for those who were "born with it." The traits that are the raw materials of leadership can be acquired. Link them up with desire and nothing can keep you from becoming a leader. This workbook will supply the leadership principles. You must supply the desire.

Leonard Ravenhill in "The Last Days Newsletter" tells about a group of tourists who were visiting a picturesque village. As they walked by an old man sitting beside a fence, one tourist asked in a patronizing way, "Were any great men born in this village?"

The old man replied, "Nope, only babies."

Leadership is developed, not discovered. The truly "born leader" will always emerge; but to stay on top, natural leadership characteristics must be developed. In working with thousands of people wanting to become leaders, I have discovered they all fit in one of four categories, or levels, of leadership:

The *Leading* Leader:

- Is born with leadership qualities

- Has seen leadership modeled throughout life.

- Has learned added leadership through training.

- Has self-discipline to become a great leader.

    Note: Three out of four of these qualities are acquired.

The *Learned* Leader:

- Has seen leadership modeled most of life.

- Has learned leadership through training.

- Has self-discipline to be a great leader.

    Note: All three qualities are acquired.

The *Latent* Leader:

- Has just recently seen leadership modeled.

- Is learning to be a leader through training.

- Has self-discipline to become a good leader.

    Note: All three qualities are acquired.

The *Limited* Leader:

- Has little or no exposure to leaders.

- Has little or no exposure to leadership training.

- Has desire to become a leader.

OBSERVATIONS

There are very few leadership books; most deal with management. There seems to be a great deal of confusion over the difference between leadership and management.

John W. Gardner, former secretary of the U.S. Department of Health, Education, and Welfare, who directed a leadership study project in Washington, D.C., pinpointed five characteristics that set "leader managers" apart from "run-of-the-mill managers."[1]

1. Leader managers are long-term thinkers who see beyond the day's crises and the quarterly report.

2. Leader managers' interests in their companies do not stop with the units they head. They want to know how all of the company's departments affect one another, and they are constantly reaching beyond their specific areas of influence.

3. Leader managers put heavy emphasis on vision, values, and motivation.

4. Leader managers have strong political skills to cope with conflicting requirements of multiple constituents.

5. Leader managers don't accept the status quo.

Management is the process of assuring that the program and objectives of the organization are implemented. Leadership, on the other hand, has to do with casting vision and motivating people.

"People don't want to be managed. They want to be led. Whoever heard of a world manager? World leader, yes. Education leader, yes. Political leader. Religious leader. Scout leader. Community leader. Labor leader. Business leader. Yes. They lead. They don't manage. The carrot always wins over the stick. Ask your horse. You can lead your horse to water, but you can't manage him to drink. If you want to manage somebody, manage yourself. Do that well and you'll be ready to stop managing and start leading."[2]

My desire is that you will be able to accomplish the work of a leader. This workbook is dedicated to that goal. Throughout the next ten weeks, you will start to discover and develop the leader within you!

This workbook will challenge you to raise your leadership lid. For about fifteen to twenty minutes each weekday you will discover and begin to apply dynamic leadership principles in your life. Simply reading my book on leadership only introduces you to new perspectives and insights. But working your way through this manual will give you a hands-on and practical approach to

- Uncovering where you are right now as a leader.

- Revealing your own assumptions and operating principles that may actually be counterproductive to your desire to lead.

- Learning new principles that work in leadership.

- Applying these principles right away in your attitudes and actions.

Each week will present a new aspect of leadership and build on the previous lessons.

In every age there comes a time when leadership must come forth to meet the needs of the hour. Therefore, there is no potential leader who does not find his or her time. Use this workbook to seize your moment!

John C. Maxwell

Week 1

The Definition of Leadership: *Influence*

INTRODUCTION

Everyone talks about it; few understand it. Most people want it; few achieve it. There are more than fifty definitions and descriptions of it in my personal files. What is this intriguing subject we call "leadership"?

Perhaps because most of us want to be leaders, we become emotionally involved when trying to define leadership. Or perhaps because we know one, we try to copy his or her behavior and describe leadership as a personality. Ask ten people to define leadership and you'll probably receive ten different answers.

How would you complete this sentence?

Leadership is

After more than four decades of observing leadership within my family and many years of developing my own leadership potential, I have come to this conclusion: *Leadership is influence.* That's it. Nothing more; nothing less. My favorite leadership proverb is: He who thinketh he leadeth and hath no one following him is only taking a walk.

1

James C. Georges of the ParTraining Corporation said, "Once you define leadership as the ability to get followers, you work backward from that point of reference to figure out how to lead."[1]

Most people define leadership as the ability to achieve a position, not the ability to get followers. Therefore, they go after a position, rank, or title, and upon their arrival they think they have become a leader. This type of thinking creates two common problems: Those who possess the "status" of a leader often experience the frustration of having few followers, and those who lead but lack the proper titles may not see themselves as leaders and therefore don't develop their leadership skills.

My goal with this workbook is to help you accept leadership as influence (that is, the ability to get followers), and then work backward from that point to help you learn how to lead. Each week is designed to place in your hand another principle that will assist your leadership development.

This first week is designed to expand your amount of *influence*. As you explore the concept that *leadership is influence*, keep in mind these key insights:

1. **Everyone influences someone.**

   To illustrate this in your life, take a moment now to jot down a few names:

   List the People You Lead   **List the People You Follow**

   Tim Elmore shared this amazing statistic with me: Sociologists tell us that even the most introverted individual will influence ten thousand other people during his or her lifetime! Tim and I concluded that each one of us is both influencing and being influenced by others. That means that all of us are leading in some areas, while in other areas we are being led. No one is excluded from being a leader or a follower. Realizing your potential as a leader is your responsibility.

2. **We never know who or how much we influence.**

   J. R. Miller said: "There have been meetings of only a moment which have left impressions for life, for eternity. No one can understand that mysterious thing we call influence . . . yet . . . every one of us continually exerts influence, either to heal, to bless, to leave marks of beauty; or to wound, to hurt, to poison, to stain other lives."[2]

3. **The best investment in the future is a proper influence today.**
   The issue is not whether you will influence someone. What needs to be settled is
   what kind of an influencer will you be? Will you grow in your leadership skills?
   In the book *Leaders*, Bennis and Nanus say, "The truth is that leadership opportunities are plentiful and within reach of most people."[3]

4. **Influence is a skill that can be developed.**
   Robert Dilenschneider, the former CEO of Hill and Knowlton, a worldwide public relations agency, has been one of the nation's major influence brokers. He
   skillfully weaves his persuasive magic in the global arena where governments and
   megacorporations meet. He wrote a book titled *Power and Influence* in which he
   shares the idea of the "power triangle" to help leaders get ahead. He says, "The
   three components of this triangle are communication, recognition, and influence. You start to communicate effectively. This leads to recognition and recognition in turn leads to influence."[4]

For years I have believed that we can increase our influence and, therefore, our leadership potential. Out of this conviction I have developed a teaching tool to assist others
in understanding their levels of leadership so they can increase their levels of influence.

This week you will

- explore the five levels of leadership:

  Day 1: Position
  Day 2: Permission
  Day 3: Production
  Day 4: People development
  Day 5: Personhood

- discover what it takes to be a leader on each level

  Read through the chart, "The Five Levels of Leadership," and then start your
  daily study.

THE FIVE LEVELS OF LEADERSHIP

5
PERSONHOOD

4
PEOPLE DEVELOPMENT

Respect
People follow because of who you are and what you represent.

NOTE: This step is reserved for leaders who have spent years growing people and organizations. Few make it. Those who do are bigger than life.

Reproduction
People follow because of what you have done for them.

NOTE: This is where long-range growth occurs. Your commitment to developing leaders will insure ongoing growth to the organization and to people. Do whatever you can to achieve and stay on this level.

3
PRODUCTION

Results
People follow because of what you have done for the organization.

NOTE: This is where success is sensed by most people. They like you and what you are doing. Problems are fixed with very little effort because of momentum.

2
PERMISSION

Relationships
People follow because they want to.

NOTE: People will follow you beyond your stated authority. This level allows work to be fun. Caution: Staying too long on this level without rising will cause highly motivated people to become restless.

1
POSITION

Rights
People follow because they have to.

NOTE: Your influence will not extend beyond the lines of your job description. The longer you stay here, the higher the turnover and the lower the morale.

Day 1

Leadership Level 1:
Position

The first level of leadership is *Position*. This is the basic entry level of leadership. The only influence you have is that which comes with a title. People who stay at this level get into territorial rights, protocol, tradition, and organizational charts. These things are not negative unless they become the sole basis for authority and influence, but they are poor substitutes for leadership skills.

What position(s) do you currently hold?

Complete these sentences:

My title is

My position is

My job description is

A person may be "in charge" because he has been appointed to a position. In that position he may have authority. But real leadership is more than having authority; it is more than having technical training and following proper procedures. Real leadership is being the person others will gladly and confidently follow. A real leader knows the difference between being the boss and being the leader.

Circle the sentences that best describe your leadership style:

A	B
I drive others.	I coach others.
I depend on authority.	I depend on goodwill.
I inspire fear.	I inspire enthusiasm.
I often say "I."	I often say "we."
I affix the blame for a breakdown.	I fix the breakdown.
I know how it is done.	I show how it is done.
I say "go."	I say "let's go!"

Which has more circles, column A or column B?

Column A represents "the boss." Column B represents "the leader." If you circled more phrases under the letter A, you may tend to lead by position.

Characteristics of a "Positional Leader"

We all display leadership characteristics. By recognizing and improving weak traits and tendencies we become better leaders.

Answer and Evaluate:

Do you feel confident in your role at work?

For a positional leader security is based on title, not talent. Since a title is arbitrary and usually bestowed by others, its security is fleeting, at best.

Were you appointed to a position or did you earn influence in the organization?

The positional level is often gained by appointment. It might not be at all based on ability, so it carries little influence.

How is your team's morale? High or low?

People will not follow a positional leader beyond his stated authority. They will do only what they have to do when they are required to do it. Thus, low morale is always present.

Do you find that you can easily influence a variety of people?

Positional leaders have more difficulty working with volunteers, white-collar workers, and younger people. Volunteers don't have to work in the organization, so there is no monetary leverage that a positional leader can use to make them respond. White-collar workers are used to participating in decision-making and resent legislative leadership. The younger generation tends to be unimpressed with mere symbols of authority.

Most of us have been taught that leadership is a position. Frustration rises within us when we get out into the real world and find that few people follow us because of our titles. Our joy and success in leading others depend on our abilities to keep climbing the levels of leadership.

APPLYING WHAT I'VE LEARNED

Now that you understand the characteristics of a positional leader, take some time to evaluate how positional you are:

- Is your leadership based on a title? If your title was taken away, how much would people still listen to you?

- Do you use the clout of your position to get others to follow? (i.e. "Because I'm the manager, that's why.") If you find that you are leading from position, pay particular attention to the Permission Level explained in tomorrow's lesson.

The following qualities are needed to be successful on the Position Level. Complete the following tasks in order to solidify your grasp of this first level.

1. **Know your job description thoroughly.**
    Write out your job description based on what you actually do every day. Then obtain your "official" job description from your organization. Are there differences in the two descriptions? Are you doing more or less?

2. **Be aware of the history of the organization, and relate the organization's history to your people (in other words, be a team player).**
    Obtain information on your organization. If you cannot find printed information, take someone who has a significant history in the organization to lunch, and ask questions. Determine the vision of your organization and the mission statement. Then use past achievements to motivate your people toward future goals. Include them in the vision of the organization, and let them know about major changes. Point out how their efforts affect the continued success of the organization.

3. **Accept responsibility, do your work with consistent excellence, and do more than is expected.**
    Take personal ownership of your work. This means your attitude shouldn't be "this is something I have to do," but rather "this is something I *can* do, and do well." Approach your tasks as challenges that you want to conquer. Ask yourself, "Is good enough good enough?" You want to take your work to the next level. You don't want to just get by, and this means going the extra mile.

4. **Offer creative ideas for change and improvement.**
    Take at least thirty minutes today to brainstorm about your work and your team. What needs improvement? What area of your work should change? Write down your ideas. Now, focus on the solutions. It's not hard to tell what is wrong. It is challenging to tell what should be done, and then do it. Pick one idea from your list and work on implementing the solution this week.

Day 2

Leadership Level 2:
Permission

"Leadership is getting people to work for you when they are not obligated," says Fred Smith. This will only happen when you climb to the second level of influence. In my book *Be a People Person*, I continually emphasize that people don't care how much you know until they know how much you care. <u>Leadership begins with the heart, not the head.</u> It flourishes with a meaningful relationship, not more regulations.

Leaders on the Position Level often lead by intimidation. They are like the chickens that Norwegian psychologist T. Schjelderup-Ebbe studied when developing the "pecking order" principle, which today is used to describe all types of social gatherings. Schjelderup-Ebbe found that in any flock one hen usually dominates all the others. She can peck any other without being pecked in return. Second comes a hen that pecks all but the top hen, and the rest are arranged in a descending hierarchy, ending in one hapless hen that is pecked by all and can peck no one.

Describe the true "pecking order" in the workplace or organization in which you are a leader. (It may or may not match the organization's formal hierarchy.)

How does this "pecking order" affect you, your team, and the organization?

A person on the Permission Level leads by interrelationships. The agenda is not the pecking order, but personal relationships. On this level, time, energy, and focus are placed on the individual's needs and desires.

From Amitai Etzioni's book *Modern Organizations* we learn the importance of meeting people's needs: "[Henry Ford] made a perfect car, the Model T, that ended the need for any other car. He was totally product-oriented. He wanted to fill the world with Model T cars. But when people started coming to him and saying, 'Mr. Ford, we'd like a different color car,' he remarked, 'You can have any color you want as long as it's black.' And that's when the decline started."

List five of the people you lead:

1.

2.

3.

4.

5.

How well do you know them? What are they interested in? Where do they spend their free time? What is their greatest concern or obligation?

Go back and write next to each name at least one need that person has. Are you meeting these needs? Highlight the names and needs that you have not yet addressed. This week, try to meet at least one person's need on the highlighted list.

People who are unable to build solid, lasting relationships will soon discover that they are unable to sustain effective leadership. Week 7 of this workbook, "Developing Your Most Appreciable Asset: People," will deal more extensively with this subject. Needless to say, you can love people without leading them, but you cannot lead people without loving them.

Many people try to skip the Permission Level and move straight on to Production. Don't. One day while I was teaching my staff the five levels of leadership, Dan Reiland shared an insight with me that I have never forgotten: "If level 1, *Position*, is the door to leadership, then level 2, *Permission*, is the foundation." Without a strong foundation, your work will not be able to stand on its own.

APPLYING WHAT I'VE LEARNED

Having lasting and trusting relationships with your workers is vital to being an effective leader. Knowing people's interests and obligations is a good starting point. As you climb the ladder of leadership, the number of people with whom you will be personally involved decreases. In order to maintain a relationship with your workers rather than maintaining a position, you need to spend time with them.

- Get to know the names and faces of your workers. (I have a Polaroid picture taken of each new employee. Listed under the picture is their name, department, and job title. This helps me to recognize people on the few days that I am in the office.)

- Provide a way for your staff to communicate to you directly, either in written or verbal form. (I read every letter and note that I receive from my staff. Many of my key leaders will E-mail a note to my assistant, which she then faxes to me whether I'm at home or at a conference.)

- Know the personal backgrounds of your workers. (I try to remember at least one unique thing about each person on my team.)

- Talk with people. (Each month I take a walk through our offices, with the goal of talking with people in every department, at every job level.)

- Make an effort to spend time with your workers personally. (The major events I attend are the company picnic and the Christmas party. This gives me the opportunity to meet the spouses and children of the people who work at my company.)

The following qualities are needed to be successful on the Permission Level. Study them, and complete the tasks under each.

1. **Possess a genuine love for people.**
   Think about how much you benefit from the people on your team. Resolve any past feelings of frustration or disappointment with your team members. Remember: "Yesterday ended last night."

2. **Make those who work with you more successful.**
   Put people in a position to win. Make a list of your team members' strengths. In what area would each person strive? Give assignments according to your team members' strengths and talents.

3. **See through other people's eyes.**
   Ask the people on your team for their opinions about a task you are currently working on. What is their perspective? Understand that each person may see the task differently depending on their involvement, past experience, and relationships with others on the team. By keeping an open mind, you can benefit from the variety of opinions.

4. **Love people more than procedures.**
   How did you react the last time one of your team members was late to work due to a family crisis or car trouble? How did your response affect your relationship with that person? You should believe in the person more than the policy. Bureaucrats don't make good leaders.

5. **Do win-win or don't do it.**
   Do you spend more time on work that benefits the team or work that benefits yourself? You should always approach a team effort with a win-win mentality. If it's only good for you don't do it. If it's only good for one other person on the team don't do it. Your team efforts should benefit the team.

6. **Include others in your journey.**

   Take someone with you. Who do you share your goals with? Who are you invest-ing in? You should have at least one person on your team that you are mentoring and sharing success with. (We will talk more about this in Week 7.)

7. **Deal wisely with difficult people.**

   If one of your team members is not contributing to the rest of the team, discuss the problem with the person one-on-one. See if the person wants to contribute, and if they do, help them get back on track.

Day 3

Leadership Level 3:
Production ✗ *I think I'm here.*

On the third level of leadership, things begin to happen, good things. Profit increases. Morale is high. Turnover is low. Needs are being met. Goals are being realized. Accompanying this growth is the "big mo"—momentum. Leading and influencing others is fun. Problems are solved with minimum effort. Fresh statistics are shared on a regular basis with the people who undergird the growth of the organization. Everyone is results-oriented. In fact, results are the main reason for the activity.

This is a major difference between levels 2 and 3. On the relationship level, people get together just to get together. There may be no other objective. On the results level, people come together to accomplish a purpose. They like to get together to get together, but they love to get together to accomplish something worthwhile. In other words, they are results-oriented.

Think about the last meeting you had at work. What was the topic? Did everyone contribute? Did you meet just to meet, or were there measurable positive results?

To move from the Permission Level to the Production Level there has to be a goal, something to work towards. People follow production leaders because of what they accomplish. People are drawn to success and want to be part of a successful project.

Recall your personal experience with a former leader.

Describe your relationship with this person:

Did you enjoy being around this leader? Why or why not?

How did this person inspire you to work harder to achieve certain goals?

Notice how the *Production* Level benefits from the *Permission* Level. People might be willing to work with a successful project leader, but without a relationship they will jump out of the way if the project starts to fail.

A leader at the Production Level is good at getting results. However, a leader should always be aware that results are not the end goal. There are more steps for a leader to climb in order to be the best he can be.

APPLYING WHAT I'VE LEARNED

What kind of track record do you have in getting things done? Specifically, how successful were your last three projects? Can you name any people who follow you because of your past successes?

To improve in the area of production, take the following steps:

1. **Initiate and accept responsibility for growth.**
   The key to improving your team is to improve yourself. How can you grow as a leader? Select resources that will help your leadership improve. How can your people grow with you? Start with this workbook. As you learn these leadership principles, teach them to your team.

2. **Develop and follow a statement of purpose.**

    If you haven't done so recently, write out your personal statement of purpose. Make sure you think about: why you are at this company, why you are in this particular job, and what you hope to accomplish during your lifetime. Once you have written your statement of purpose, determine whether you are following it.

3. **Develop a system of accountability for results, beginning with yourself.**

    Ask a trusted colleague for input on your work performance. This week, make a list of the tasks you are working on. On Friday, take time to review what you accomplished. What items did you check off? Encourage your team members to do the same self-evaluation on a regular basis.

4. **Know and do the things that give a high return.**

    Look at your to do list and rank your tasks in order of importance. Then focus 80 percent of you time on the top 20 percent of your tasks. (I'll explain more about this in Week 2.)

5. **Communicate the strategy and vision of the organization.**

    How long has it been since you spent time casting vision with your people? Meet with your group and go over what you have done, what you are doing now, and what you want to accomplish in the future. You should never *assume* your people are on the same page as you.

6. **Make the difficult decisions that will make a difference.**

    Today, make one tough decision. It could be something that you have been putting off for a while. Collect your thoughts and information about the situation, and go for it. Over the next few days, track the results of your decision. Was it worth it? Did it move you and your team forward?

Day 4

Leadership Level 4:
People Development

How do you spot a leader? We certainly would look for characteristics like strength and influence. However, most leaders have weaknesses as well as strengths. Since every leader is different, the true leader can be recognized because somehow or other his people consistently demonstrate superior performance.

A leader is great, not because of his or her power, but because of the ability to empower others. Success without a successor is failure. A worker's main responsibility is doing the work himself. A leader's main responsibility is developing others to do the work.

True or false:

If you want something done right, you have to do it yourself. ___

False. The only time it's true is when the task is so specific to your gifts that you are the only person who *can* do the job. However, for the leader who is making decisions and delegating duties, the above mentality often leads to unmotivated and insecure workers. Your task as a leader is to help people develop into solid and confident workers, who are able to take on responsibilities with confidence. If you want something done right, give it to a person you have trained and invested in.

Loyalty to the leader reaches its peak when the follower has personally grown through the mentorship of the leader. Note the progression: At level 2, the follower loves the leader; at level 3, the follower admires the leader; at level 4, the follower is loyal to the leader. Why? You win people's hearts by helping them grow personally.

What is a mentor? A mentor is a person who embodies the characteristics that you admire, *and* is willing to help you develop those characteristics yourself, so you can achieve your goals and ambitions.

Write down the names of three mentors you have had in your life, and next to the names list the qualities that they helped you develop.

Mentor	Qualities
1.	
2.	
3.	

If you are leading others, then it is time for you to become the mentor. The core of leaders who surround you should all be people you personally touch or help to develop in some way. When that happens, love and loyalty will be exhibited by those closest to you and by those who are touched by your key leaders.

APPLYING WHAT I'VE LEARNED

The following qualities and suggestions will help you become a better people developer:

A Successful People Developer

1. Realizes that people are his or her most valuable asset.

2. Places a priority on developing people.

3. Becomes a model for others to follow.

4. Pours leadership efforts into the top 20 percent of his or her people.

5. Exposes key leaders to growth opportunities.

6. Is able to attract other winners/producers to the common goal.

7. Surrounds himself or herself with an inner core that complements his or her leadership.

To Develop Key Leaders:

I systematically meet with and teach those who are influencers within my organization. They in turn pass on to others what I have given them. As you influence and lead others, they will learn what it means to be a leader. Your influence, therefore, does not end with you. It carries on long after you have gone.

To implement a people-developer leadership style, you will need to make some decisions concerning what you can do. First, choose who you will mentor. Second, find ways to help develop those people.

Get started by including them in one of the following:

1. Mentoring Groups. Invite them into a small group that you spend time with on a regular basis.

2. Resources. As you read books, hear tapes, or view resources that especially help you, pass them on to your people.

3. Conferences. Take individuals or a group along to significant conferences.

You can begin to put into practice the ways you are going to develop people today. Remember that they are looking to you to guide them, not to do the work for them. It's your job to help raise them to the next level. You should set aside time on your calendar to meet with these people. At this level, developing others is a priority.

Day 5

Leadership Level 5: *Personhood*

The fifth level of leadership, *personhood,* is the level that can be achieved only through extreme dedication, personal vision, and hard work. Only a lifetime of proven leadership will allow us to sit at level 5 and reap the rewards that are eternally satisfying.

Personhood is a level reserved for those few who have spent years growing people and organizations. The key characteristic of leaders who have achieved personhood is respect. People follow leaders here because of who they are and what they represent. They are admired and followed not because of their position, but because of their disposition.

List a few leaders from your lifetime that you feel have achieved the level of personhood:

Example: *Mother Teresa*

We respect these individuals not only for what they have accomplished, but also for who they have become. They have shaped our ideas and our understandings and have maintained a profound connection to the people that they mentor. Few will reach this level, but it is attainable.

APPLYING WHAT I'VE LEARNED

The following phrases reflect the success of someone on the Personhood Level:

- Your followers are loyal and sacrificial.

- You have spent years mentoring and molding leaders.

- You have become a statesman/consultant; others seek you out.

- Your greatest joy comes from watching others grow and develop.

- Your influence transcends that of the organization.

You cannot place yourself on the Personhood Level. Only others can do that. The best you can do is dedicate yourself to working your way up through the levels of leadership. Reach the People Development Level with as many people as you can. Do that for a lifetime, and you just might find yourself living on the highest level.

CONCLUSIONS ON INFLUENCE

Everyone is a leader because everyone influences someone. Not everyone will become a great leader, but everyone can become a better leader. Now you've been given a blueprint to help you understand influence and how to increase it.

Keys to influence:

1. *Know what level you are leading from.* You will be on different levels with different people. Observe your interactions this week to determine what level you are on with each person on your team.

2. *Know and apply the qualities needed to be successful at each level.* The more intentional you are about being a leader, the more success you will have in winning people's respect and cooperation.

INFLUENCE
DISCUSSION QUESTIONS

1. This week you read that leadership is influence. Describe some of the ways that you think most people on the street would define leadership if you were to ask them. How would they describe it?

2. Think about the different bosses (or coaches, ministry leaders, teachers, etc.) that you've had in the past. How would you describe the worst one? How about the best one? What were the greatest differences?

3. Why is positional leadership considered to be the lowest level of leadership?

4. Most people who grow beyond the "Position" level of leadership tend to be naturally better at either "Permission" or "Production." Which is your greater strength and why?

5. If you were given a position of leadership in a new area of responsibility where you had little experience and no track record, how would you go about building the relationships needed to move up to the Permission Level with others? If you have had experience with that kind situation in the past, please describe what you did and whether you were successful.

6. What is the key to success on the "Production" level of leadership? *goal*

7. Why can't a person skip a level and still be effective as a leader?

8. Moving from the "Production" to the "People Development" level of leadership is often very difficult for most leaders. Why do you think that is? *rely on self for achievements*

9. Have you benefited from the mentoring of a leader who developed people? If so, describe the experience.

10. If you judge your leadership according to your level of influence you have with others, then how would you describe yourself?
    A) People flock to me and genuinely desire to follow me.
    B) When I desire to get people to follow me, they gladly do it.
    C) I have influence with only a few people, and have little success as a leader.
    D) I'm on my own—no one is willingly following me.

11. What must you do to become better at leading on the next level?

Week 2

The Key to Leadership:
Priorities

INTRODUCTION

Let's begin this week by talking about a key word for any endeavor—*success*. How do you define *success*?

Success is

Success can be defined as *the progressive realization of a predetermined goal.* This definition tells us that the discipline to prioritize and the ability to work toward a stated goal are essential to a leader's success. In fact, I believe prioritizing is the key to personal effectiveness.

While attending a conference, I heard a speaker say, "There are two things that are most difficult to get people to do: to think and to do things in order of importance." He went on to say that these two things are the difference between a professional and an amateur.

I also believe that thinking ahead and prioritizing responsibilities mark the major differences between a leader and a follower because:

- Practical people know how to get what they want.

- Philosophers know what they ought to want.

- Leaders know how to get what they ought to want.

Prioritizing comes naturally for many people. For some, however, it is tremendously difficult knowing exactly what to do and how to do it in order of importance. Someone may feel that he has worked very hard on a particular task, but if the results produced do not meet expectations, then that person may have worked inefficiently.

How much time did you spend on your last work assignment? Did the end result reflect the effort you put forth? If not, why?

At a time when people expect things better, faster, and cheaper, a good leader should know how to prioritize and increase efficiency within his organization.

This week we will explore the world of priorities. How well you prioritize your time, money, resources, and team will determine how successful your organization will be. We will be looking at the following categories:

- Efficiency for survival

- Organize or agonize

- Evaluate or stalemate

- Understanding what's important

- You can't have it all

Each day will help you evaluate how efficient you and your organization are, and you will learn how to make improvements. No matter how large or small your organization, prioritizing will enable you to work smarter, to increase productivity, and enhance your performance.

Start off by listing some areas within your own work that you think could be more efficient:

1. meetings
2. EE interactions
3. HR Team interaction
4. the things I don't want to do
5. the things that require quiet time

Throughout this week, refer to this list to see if you have learned some techniques for improving efficiency in these areas. More often than not, applying simple principles can increase efficiency.

Day 1

Efficiency for Survival

Many years ago, while working toward a business degree, I learned about the Pareto Principle. It is commonly called the 20/80 principle. Although I received little information about this principle at the time, I began applying it to my life. All of these years later, I find it's still a useful tool for determining priorities for my life and organization.

THE PARETO PRINCIPLE

20 percent of your priorities will give you 80 percent
of your production,
IF
you spend your time, energy, money, and personnel
on the top 20 percent of your priorities.

Here are some examples:

- **Time:** 20 percent of our time produces 80 percent of the results.

- **Products:** 20 percent of the products bring in 80 percent of the profit.

- **Reading:** 20 percent of the book contains 80 percent of the content.

- **Job:** 20 percent of our work gives us 80 percent of our satisfaction.

- **Speech:** 20 percent of the presentation produces 80 percent of the impact.

- **Funds:** 20 percent of the people will give 80 percent of the money.

- **Leadership:** 20 percent of the people will make 80 percent of the decisions.

Every leader needs to understand the Pareto Principle in the area of people oversight and leadership. For example, 20 percent of the people in an organization will be responsible for 80 percent of the organization's success. This is simply the way it works.

The following strategy will enable a leader to increase the productivity of an organization:

1. Determine which people are the top 20 percent producers.

❑ _____

❑ _____

❑ _____

❑ _____

❑ _____

❑ _____

❑ _____

❑ _____

❑ _____

2 Spend 80 percent of your "people time" with the top 20 percent.

3. Spend 80 percent of your personal developmental dollars on the top 20 percent.

4. Determine what 20 percent of the work gives 80 percent of the return, and train an assistant to do the other 80 percent less-effective work. This "frees up" the producer to do what he does best.

5. Ask the top 20 percent to do on-the-job training for the next 20 percent.

Efficiency is the foundation for survival. Effectiveness is the foundation for success. Being able to prioritize your personnel, time, and energy will allow you the freedom to produce more efficient results. Remember, we teach what we know; we reproduce what we are. Like begets like.

Here is the way to identify the top 20 percent influencers/producers in your organization:

1. Make a list of everyone in your organization or department.

2. For each individual, ask yourself, "If this person takes a negative action against me or withdraws his or her support from me, how big will the impact be?"

3. If their absence would hinder your ability to function, put a check mark next to that name. If the person would not make or break you in terms of your ability to accomplish important tasks, don't check their name. (Additional spaces may be required.)

When you finish making the check marks, you will have marked between 15 and 20 percent of the names. (If you used all 10 blanks above, you should have marked one or two names.) These are the vital relationships that need to be developed and given the proper amount of resources to grow the organization.

Many potentially great leaders remain unsuccessful simply because they are inefficient. By knowing where you should spend your time and energy, you'll be more focused, and the more results you will see.

APPLYING WHAT I'VE LEARNED

Work on your 20/80 lists in other areas:

1. Make a list of the tasks you are working on or overseeing. What is your most important task? Are you spending at least 80 percent of your time on it? You may need to keep track of the hours you spend on each task this week, and at the end of the week determine if you are using your time efficiently. Delegate less important tasks, especially those which took up more than 20 percent of your time.

2. Meet one-on-one with the people you checked above. Ask for their insight on who they would consider their top 20 percent (who are the people they consider leaders or influencers beneath them in the organization). Add these names to your list beside the name of the person who mentioned them. As you start developing your top 20 percent, encourage them to develop their top 20 percent.

Day 2

Organize or Agonize

Most of us would consider ourselves hard workers. Just being in a position of leadership requires hard work and an understanding of the duties, but what happens if a leader is unable to organize himself or his duties? Probably a lot of energy will be expended, with few results. Ultimately it's not how hard you work; it's how smart you work.

The ability to juggle three or four high-priority tasks successfully is a must for every leader. A life in which anything goes will ultimately be a life in which nothing goes. A first step toward organizing is to prioritize your assignments. Here are several categories you can use to organize your work:

- *High Importance/High Urgency:* Tackle these tasks first.

- *High Importance/Low Urgency:* Set deadlines for completion and get these tasks worked into your daily routine.

- *Low Importance/High Urgency:* Find quick, efficient ways to get this work done without much personal involvement. Delegate it to a "can do" assistant.

- *Low Importance/Low Urgency:* This is busy or repetitive work such as filing. Stack it up and do it in one-half hour segments every week; get somebody else to do it; or don't do it at all. Before putting off until tomorrow something you can do today, study it clearly. Maybe you can postpone it indefinitely.

Now, take a few moments and think about tasks that you have for today, this week, and the near future. Place each task in the appropriate box. This should help you identify the tasks that have the highest priority and the jobs that can wait.

High Importance/High Urgency	High Importance/Low Urgency
Low Importance/High Urgency	Low Importance/Low Urgency

You must choose what you will do with your time and energy. Every person is either an initiator or a reactor when it comes to planning. An example is our calendars. The question is not, "Will my calendar be full?" but "Who will fill my calendar?" If we are leaders of others, the question is not "Will I see people?" but "Who will I see?" My observation is that leaders tend to initiate and followers tend to react.

ARE YOU AN INITIATOR OR A REACTOR?

1. **Do you tend to make calls or answer calls during the day?**

   A leader makes contact. He is not waiting for the phone to ring, because he is too busy calling the people on his top 20 percent list. This list doesn't just consist of the catalysts *within* your organization. This list includes people outside of your organization that might help you in reaching your goals.

   If you don't already have a contact list, take time to make one.

2. **Do you spend time planning and anticipating problems, or do you take things as they come?**

A leader is rarely surprised. He is thinking ahead. By preparing for the worst, he doesn't have to stop completely when a challenge arises. His reaction has already been thought out; therefore, his solution isn't a shot in the dark.

List roadblocks you could encounter in achieving your most important goal. Ask for suggestions and insight from others to ensure you have full understanding of the possibilities.

3. **When you are with others, are you intentionally investing in them?**

A leader invests in people. He seldom meets with anyone without having a plan. At every opportunity whether a ballgame or business lunch he is making contact and developing his people.

Investing in others should be a priority. Find ways to connect with and develop your top 20 percent. Share your wisdom and insight. Listen to their thoughts and ideas. Recommend books they should read. Share with them ways you overcame challenges. Let them in on your "secrets to success."

4. **How do you fill your calendar?**

A leader fills his calendar according to priorities. A leader's time is limited, yet as he advances through the levels of leadership, more people ask for his time. He must take control of this area, or he will be controlled by it.

Look at your calendar and determine if you are filling your days by request or by priority. You should eliminate events that do not relate to your goals and objectives. Writing everything on your calendar (including meetings, dinners, scheduled phone calls, family time) will help you to prioritize.

A true leader must be intentional about priorities. Efficiency requires thought and anticipation. It requires the leader to constantly be thinking ahead. A leader without vision can't lead very far.

APPLYING WHAT I'VE LEARNED

A few years ago I was teaching the 20/80 principle at a conference in Boston. A few weeks later my friend John Bowen sent me a tablet of paper that he designed from the lecture. I have used it for my own prioritizing ever since. Perhaps it will have value to you, too. To end today's exercise, take a few minutes and fill out the Pareto list for tomorrow. Then see how well the rest of your week flows with this type of prioritizing.

PARETO

DATE _____

<table>
<tr><td>PHONE CALLS TO MAKE</td><td>COMP</td></tr>
<tr><td>1. _____</td><td>☐</td></tr>
<tr><td>2. _____</td><td>☐</td></tr>
<tr><td>3. _____</td><td>☐</td></tr>
<tr><td>4. _____</td><td>☐</td></tr>
</table>

<table>
<tr><td>PERSONAL NOTES</td><td>COMP</td></tr>
<tr><td>1. _____</td><td>☐</td></tr>
<tr><td>2. _____</td><td>☐</td></tr>
<tr><td>3. _____</td><td>☐</td></tr>
<tr><td>4. _____</td><td>☐</td></tr>
</table>

20/80 TIME

ORDER OF PRIORITY   **TIME ALLOWED**   **DESCRIPTION**—List of things to do <u>now</u>   **COMPLETED**
(High importance; <u>high</u> urgency)

1. _____ ☐
2. _____ ☐
3. _____ ☐
4. _____ ☐
5. _____ ☐
6. _____ ☐
7. _____ ☐
8. _____ ☐
9. _____ ☐
10. _____ ☐

LIST OF THINGS TO DO
(High importance; low urgency)

1. _____ ☐
2. _____ ☐
3. _____ ☐
4. _____ ☐
5. _____ ☐
6. _____ ☐
7. _____ ☐
8. _____ ☐

LIST OF THINGS TO DELEGATE
(Low importance; high urgency)

1. _____ ☐
2. _____ ☐
3. _____ ☐
4. _____ ☐
5. _____ ☐
6. _____ ☐
7. _____ ☐
8. _____ ☐

Day 3

Evaluate or Stalemate

A veteran of many years of decision-making gave me this short, simple advice: Decide what to do, and do it. Decide what not to do, and don't do it. Evaluation of priorities, however, is not quite that simple. Many times they are not black or white, but many tones of gray. I have found that the last thing one knows is what to put first.

Today, you will be considering several questions to assist you in the priority process:

WHAT IS REQUIRED OF ME?

A leader can give up anything except final responsibility. The question that must always be answered before accepting a new job is "What is required of me?" In other words, what do I have to do that no one but me can do? Whatever those things are, they must be put high on the priority list. Failure to do them will cause you to be among the unemployed.

A team has many responsibilities, but the leader is rarely the one and only one who can do them. Distinguish between what you have to do and what can be delegated to someone else.

Take a minute and list what is required of you in your job (by priority, if possible):

1.

2.

3.

4.

WHAT GIVES ME THE GREATEST RETURN?

The effort expended should approximate the results expected. A question I must continually ask myself is, "Am I doing what I do best and receiving a good return for the organization?" Here are three common problems in many organizations:

- **Abuse:** Too few employees are doing too much.

- **Disuse:** Too many employees are doing too little.

- **Misuse:** Too many employees are doing the wrong things.

Bo Jackson played defensive end for his high school football team. He was good, but didn't lead his team to a championship. In fact they finished the season with three wins and seven losses. At Auburn University, when all three running backs were injured, Bo's coach asked him to fill in "until the regulars are healthy again." Bo was apprehensive, but did it. The rest is history. Jackson went on to a distinguished career as a running back in the National Football League.

List what gives you the greatest return on your job:

1.

2.

3.

4.

WHAT IS MOST REWARDING?

Life is too short not to be fun. Our best work takes place when we enjoy it. Some time ago I spoke at a leaders' conference with Ken Blanchard and we were both attempting to teach this principle. The title of my lecture was "Take This Job and Love It." I encouraged the audience to find something they liked to do so much they would gladly do it for nothing. Then I suggested they learn to do it so well that people would be happy to pay them for it. Andy Granatelli said that when you are making a success of something, it's not work—it's a way of life. You enjoy yourself because you are making your contribution to the world. I believe that!

List what is most satisfying in your job:

1.

2.

3.

4.

Success in your work will be greatly increased if the *requirements, return,* and *rewards* are similar. In other words, if the requirements of my job are the same as my strengths that give me the highest return and doing those things brings me great pleasure, then I will be successful if I act on my priorities.

APPLYING WHAT I'VE LEARNED

Hopefully, some of your answers for the above lists coincided. For example, my list might have looked like this:

> Requirement–writing lessons
> Return–a finished lesson that helped someone develop their leadership skills
> Reward–knowing that I helped to develop another leader

Review your lists, and note any recurring themes. These are the areas you need to focus on and make priorities, if you are not already doing so.

Day 4

Understanding What's Important

Priorities never "stay put." They continually shift and demand attention. H. Ross Perot said that anything that is excellent or praiseworthy stands moment-by-moment on the cutting edge and must be constantly fought for. Well-placed priorities always sit on "the edge."

To keep priorities in place:

- **Evaluate:** Every month review the 3 R's (Requirements/Return/Reward).

- **Eliminate:** Ask yourself, "What am I doing that can be done by someone else?"

- **Estimate:** What are the top projects you are doing this month and how long will they take?

YOU CANNOT OVERESTIMATE THE UNIMPORTANCE OF PRACTICALLY EVERYTHING

I love this principle. It's a little exaggerated but needs to be said. William James said that the art of being wise is "the art of knowing what to overlook." The petty and the mundane steal much of our time. Too many people are living for the wrong things.

Think back over the past. How many projects did you spend excessive energy on that, in retrospect, were really not that important? Write them down.

1. SoS

2. Surveys (comp)

3. Volunteer/charity

4.

5.

6.

7.

8.

We spend much of our time performing seemingly important tasks. But in reality, how important are the things that we do? Dr. Anthony Campolo tells about a sociological study in which fifty people over the age of ninety-five were asked one question: "If you could live your life over again, what would you do differently?" It was an open-ended question, and a number of answers came from these eldest of senior citizens. However, three answers constantly reemerged and dominated the results of the study. These three answers were:

- If I had it to do over again, I would reflect more.

- If I had it to do over again, I would risk more.

- If I had it to do over again, I would do more things that would live on after I am dead.

How would you answer this question?

If I had to do it over again, I would

be more patient... reflect more... understand my reactions - before I deliver them so I could change them.

Now, put your words into action! If you wrote that you would spend more time with your family—make that a priority. If you wrote that you would leave a legacy— find someone to invest in and become a mentor. If it was important enough to live your life over to do, shouldn't it be important enough to start doing today?

THE GOOD IS THE ENEMY OF THE BEST

Most people can prioritize when faced with right or wrong issues. The challenge arises when we are faced with two good choices. Now what should we do? What if both choices fall comfortably into the requirements, return, and reward of our work?

How to Break the Tie Between Two Good Options:

- Ask your overseer or coworkers their preference.

- Can one of the options be handled by someone else? If so, pass it on and work on the one only you can do.

- Which option would be of more benefit to the recipient? Too many times we are like the merchant who was so intent on trying to keep the store clean that he would never unlock the front door. The real reason for running the store is to have customers come in, not to clean it up!

- Make your decision based on the purpose of the organization.

Write down a recent decision you had to make between two good options.

What method did you use to make a decision? What was the outcome? As you read the following example, notice how decisions between the good and the best can have very different outcomes:

A lighthouse keeper who worked on a rocky stretch of coastline received his new supply of oil once a month to keep the light burning. Not being far from shore, he had frequent guests. One night a woman from the village begged for some oil to keep her family warm. Another time a father asked for some to use in his lamp. Another needed some to lubricate a wheel. Since all the requests seemed legitimate, the lighthouse keeper tried to please everyone and grant the requests of all. Toward the end of the month he noticed the supply of oil was very low. Soon it was gone, and the beacon went out. That night several ships were wrecked and lives were lost. When the authorities investigated, the man was very repentant. To his excuses and pleading their reply was, "You were given oil for one purpose—to keep that light burning!"

As a leader, you have a responsibility to maintain a vision for what is best. In many instances there will not be an absolute answer unless you are determined to reach your goals. What is the purpose of your tasks? Focus on it.

APPLYING WHAT I'VE LEARNED

When we are in a position of leadership, the decisions often come down to us. Choose a task that you are currently working on. Write out the primary purpose for the task. Refer to the purpose statement anytime you are asked to make a decision concerning that task.

Day 5

You Can't Have It All

When my son, Joel Porter, was young, I would tell him each time we entered a store, "You can't have it all." Like many people, he had a hard time eliminating things in his life. Ninety-five percent of achieving anything is knowing what you want. Many years ago I read this poem by William H. Hinson:

> He who seeks one thing, and but one,
> May hope to achieve it before life is done.
> But he who seeks all things wherever he goes
> Must reap around him in whatever he sows
> A harvest of barren regret.

Regret can be one of the most devastating feelings a person can have. When you attempt to do too much, you are unable to accomplish much of it, and the things that you do accomplish will tend to be mediocre.

Even when we don't desire to do everything, we still may try to tackle more than we can handle. Too many priorities paralyze us. Every one of us has looked at our desks filled with memos and papers, heard the phone ringing, and watched the door open all at the same time! Remember the "frozen feeling" that came over you?

Fill in the blank: I work _too many wasted_ **hours per week.**

Now ask yourself, "Do I work this much because I can never keep up or because I have set certain goals that I want to reach?" Many people get swamped and have to work excessively long hours. If you have set your priorities in order, then you will be able to avoid this situation. All true leaders have learned to say no to the good in order to say yes to the best.

WHEN LITTLE PRIORITIES DEMAND TOO MUCH OF US, BIG PROBLEMS ARISE

Robert J. McKain said, "The reason most major goals are not achieved is that we spend our time doing second things first." Often the little things in life trip us up. A tragic example is the Eastern Airlines jumbo jet that crashed in the Everglades of Florida. The plane was the now infamous Flight 401, bound from New York to Miami with a heavy load of holiday passengers. As the plane approached the Miami airport for its landing, the light that indicates proper deployment of the landing gear failed to come on. The plane flew in a large, looping circle over the swamps of the Everglades while the cockpit crew checked to see if the gear actually had not deployed, or if instead the bulb in the signal light was defective.

When the flight engineer tried to remove the light bulb, it wouldn't budge, and the other members of the crew tried to help him. As they struggled with the bulb, no one noticed the aircraft was losing altitude, and the plane flew right into the swamp. Dozens of people were killed in the crash. While an experienced crew of high-priced pilots worked on a seventy-five-cent light bulb, the plane with its passengers flew right into the ground.

Often, when we let simple tasks overwhelm us, we are unable to see the bigger picture. List the small, daily priorities that seem to bog you down:

As you begin to prioritize your work, try to find ways of eliminating or delegating these simpler tasks in order to maintain a focus on the larger priority.

TIME DEADLINES AND EMERGENCIES FORCE US TO PRIORITIZE

We find this in Parkinson's Law: If you have only one letter to write, it will take all day to do it. If you have twenty letters to write, you'll get them done in one day.

When is our work the most efficient? The week before vacation! Why can't we always run our lives the way we do the week before we take off? Under normal conditions, we are efficient (doing things right). When time pressure mounts or emergencies arise, we become effective (doing the right things). As I said before: Efficiency is the foundation for survival. Effectiveness is the foundation of success.

To move from Efficient to Effective: List the two or three things that would have a major impact on you or your organization if the tasks weren't completed. Concentrate your time and energy on these things. Try to delegate or eliminate the rest.

APPLYING WHAT I'VE LEARNED

Too often we learn too late what is really important. Looking back, we realize that we have spent our time on things that don't last or things that don't make a difference, and we can never relive those moments. In order to make the most of your time, you must prioritize.

Once again, eliminate unimportant tasks. You can do this on a trial basis. From the previous list, choose one thing to eliminate. If you find that its elimination hinders your work, try to delegate it to a suitable person on your team.

Set short-term goals for yourself. If you need to, find someone who will hold you accountable to those goals. Force yourself to prioritize by breaking major tasks into smaller tasks, which have to be done sooner in order to move on forward. An example would be: I will finish this task before I go to lunch, or I will finish this task before the end of the day.

PRIORITIES
DISCUSSION QUESTIONS

1. Everyone has to find a method for dealing with life's challenges. How do you decide whether something is urgent, important, or unimportant?

2. Describe some of the time management systems you have used in the past. How well have they worked for you?

3. Living by priorities involves being on the right course as well as doing the right things day to day. Think about how you spend your day. Then consider:
   A) How much of what you do is required of you? (Anything that is in line with your moral and ethical standards is a requirement. So is anything that *cannot* be delegated to anyone else.)
   B) Which activities that you do bring the greatest return, based on your talents, skills, and opportunities?
   C) What brings you the greatest reward, the most personal satisfaction based on your vision, passions, and desire?

4. If someone discovers that most of what he or she does doesn't fit into those three categories (requirement, return, reward), then major life change is often in order. What kinds of adjustments might be necessary for someone in that position?

5. Does that situation apply to you? If so, explain.

6. According to the Pareto Principle, you should spend 80 percent of your time on the top 20 percent of your duties. To apply that principle to yourself, consider your own priorities. For example, if you are responsible for five projects, then one should receive 80 percent of your time. If you have fifty clients, then ten should receive 80 percent of your attention. According to that standard, how well are you applying the Pareto Principle?

7. What kinds of changes would you have to make in order to better implement the Pareto Principle in your life?

8. It's one thing to use the Pareto Principle for arranging tasks. It's another to prioritize the time you spend with people, especially since the people with the greatest

problems want most of your time. How do you feel about spending 80 percent of your time with the top 20 percent of the people under your leadership?

9. If you focus on the top 20 percent of your people, they in turn focus on the next 20 percent, and so on, how should that benefit you as well as your entire organization?

Week 3

The Most Important Ingredient of Leadership: *Integrity*

INTRODUCTION

How do you define integrity?

Integrity is

According to Webster, *integrity* is "the state of being complete, unified." When I have integrity, my words and my deeds match up. I am who I am, no matter where I am or who I am with.

Integrity is a vanishing commodity today. Personal standards are crumbling in a world that has taken to the hot pursuit of personal pleasure and shortcuts to success.

The White House, the Pentagon, Capitol Hill, the church, the sports arena, the academy, even the day care center have all been hit hard by scandal. In every case, the lack of credibility can be traced back to the level of integrity of the individuals within those organizations and institutions.

A person with integrity does not have divided loyalties (that's duplicity), nor is he or she merely pretending (that's hypocrisy). People with integrity are "whole" people; they can be identified by their single-mindedness. People with integrity have nothing to hide and nothing to fear. Their lives are open books. The senior editor of *Christianity Today* magazine, V. Gilbert Beers, said, "A person of integrity is one who has established a system of values against which all of life is judged."

Integrity is not what we do so much as who we are. And who we are, in turn, determines what we do. Our system of values is so much a part of us we cannot separate it from ourselves. It becomes the navigating system that guides us. It establishes priorities in our lives and determines what we will accept or reject.

"The first key to greatness," Socrates reminds us, "is to be in reality what we appear to be." Too often we try to be a "human doing" before we have become a "human being." To earn trust, a leader has to be authentic. For that to happen, one must come across as a good musical composition does—the words and the music must match.

Ask yourself:

If I talk about the importance of being on time: Am I late? Are my followers late?
If I tell others to look at the bright side of things: Do I exhibit a positive attitude? Do my followers exhibit positive attitudes?
I know I need to do more than just get by: Do I show excellence in my work? Do my followers show excellence in their work?

Eighty-nine percent of what people learn comes through visual stimulation, 10 percent through audible stimulation, and one percent through other senses. So it makes sense that the more followers see and hear their leader being consistent in action and word, the greater their consistency and loyalty. *What they hear, they understand. What they see, they believe!*

This week you will be learning how integrity

- Builds trust.

- Has high influence value.

- Facilitates high standards.

- Builds solid reputation, not just image.

- Means living it before leading others.

- Helps a leader be credible, not just clever.

- Is a hard-won achievement.

As you build your life on the foundation of integrity, use the following poem as a "Mirror Test" to evaluate how you're doing.

AM I TRUE TO MYSELF?

by Edgar Guest

I have to live with myself, and so
I want to be fit for myself to know,
I want to be able, as days go by,
Always to look myself straight in the eye;
I don't want to stand, with the setting sun,
And hate myself for things I have done.
I don't want to keep on a closet shelf
A lot of secrets about myself,
And fool myself, as I come and go,
Into thinking that nobody else will know
The kind of man I really am;
I don't want to dress up myself in sham.
I want to go out with my head erect,
I want to deserve all men's respect;
But here in the struggle for fame and pelf
I want to be able to like myself.
I don't want to look at myself and know
That I'm bluster and bluff and empty show.
I can never hide myself from me;
I see what others may never see;
I know what others may never know,
I never can fool myself, and so,
Whatever happens, I want to be
Self-respecting and conscience free.

Day 1

Integrity Builds Trust

The more credible you are, the more confidence people place in you and give you the privilege of influencing their lives. The less credible you are, the less confidence people place in you, and the more quickly you lose your position of influence and leadership.

Many leaders who have attended my conferences have said to me, "I hope you can give me some insights into how I can change my company." My response is always the same: "My goal is to inspire *you* to change; if that happens, the organization will also be changed." As I have said time and time again, everything rises and falls on leadership. The secret to rising and not falling is integrity.

LEADERSHIP FUNCTIONS ON THE BASIS OF TRUST

Dwight Eisenhower said: "In order to be a leader a man must have followers. And to have followers, a man must have their confidence. Hence, the supreme quality for a leader is unquestionable integrity. Without it, no real success is possible, no matter whether it is on a section gang, a football field, in an army, or in an office. If a man's associates find him guilty of being phony, if they find that he lacks forthright integrity, he will fail. His teachings and actions must square with each other. The first great need, therefore, is integrity and high purpose."[1]

When you present a new idea to your team, how do they tend to respond?

If their response is skepticism, then you may have integrity issues. We have learned that in order to move up the five levels of leadership, we must have results. People want to win. They don't want to be deserted or lied to. What is your track record? Do your people believe you'll deliver on your promises? Are you presenting yourself as an effective leader? Make sure you can do what you say you are going to do.

Pieter Bruyn, a Dutch specialist in administration, holds that authority is not the power a boss has over subordinates, but the boss's ability to influence subordinates to recognize and accept that power. He calls it a "bargain": Subordinates tacitly agree to accept the boss as boss in return for being offered the kind of leadership *they* can accept.

What does Bruyn's theory boil down to? Quite simply the leader must build—and maintain—credibility. Subordinates must be able to trust that their boss will act in good faith toward them.

What requirements must be met for you to trust someone?

Example: *They follow through on promises.*

Too often people with leadership responsibilities look to the organization to *make* people follow them. They ask for a new title, another position, an organizational chart, or a new policy to curtail insubordination. But they never get enough authority to become effective. Why? I believe that they are looking to the outside when their problem is on the inside. They lack authority because they lack integrity.

What do you do to secure the trust of your followers?

Cavett Roberts said: "If my people understand me, I'll get their attention. If my people trust me, I'll get their action." For a leader to have the authority to lead, he needs more than the title on his door. He has to have the trust of those who are following him.

APPLYING WHAT I'VE LEARNED

Increase your trust factor. One of the best ways to show that you are trustworthy is to do something because it is the right thing to do. It may not be the easy thing to do or the most popular thing to do, but it displays integrity.

I've heard people say, "I wouldn't trust him as far as I could throw him." And many times this comment is based on the distrust of someone because they lied. Today, just be honest. Tell the truth even in the most difficult situations. Telling the truth means taking full responsibility for your actions. Focus on the areas in which you would normally avoid a question, and go for the truth.

Day 2

People Do What People See

INTEGRITY HAS HIGH INFLUENCE VALUE

Emerson said, "Every great institution is the lengthened shadow of a single man. His character determines the character of the organization." That statement "lines up" with the words of Will Rogers who said, "People's minds are changed through observation and not argument." People do what people see.

On a scale of 1 to 10, how necessary do you think integrity is to business success? According to 1,300 senior executives who responded to a survey, integrity is the human quality most necessary to business success. Seventy-one percent put it at the top of a list of sixteen traits responsible for enhancing an executive's effectiveness.[2]

INTEGRITY FACILITATES HIGH STANDARDS

Leaders are to live by a higher standard than that of their followers. This insight is exactly the opposite of most people's thoughts concerning leadership. In a world of perks and privileges that accompany the climb to success, little thought is given to the responsibilities of the upward journey.

Leaders can give up anything except responsibility, either for themselves or for their organizations. John D. Rockefeller Jr. said, "I believe that every right implies a responsibility; every opportunity, an obligation; every possession, a duty."

Think about your rise in leadership. Any time you climbed the ladder in the past:

• Did your rights increase or decrease?

• Did your responsibilities increase or decrease?

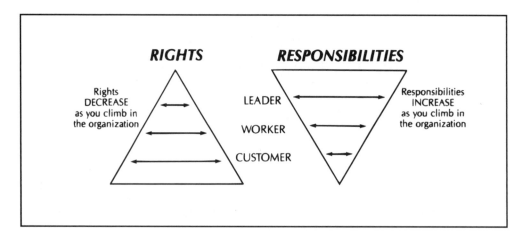

Too many people are ready to assert their rights, but not to assume their responsibilities. Richard L. Evans, in his book *An Open Road*, said: "It is priceless to find a person who will take responsibility, who will finish and follow through to the final detail—to know when someone has accepted an assignment that it will be effectively, conscientiously completed. But when half-finished assignments keep coming back—to check on, to verify, to edit, to interrupt thought, and to take repeated attention—obviously someone has failed to follow the doctrine of completed work."

Do you ever find yourself saying phrases like:

"I've earned this perk."
"It was *my* decision to make."
"That's none of your business."
"I should be able to . . ."
"I have a right to . . ."

If you find that you are talking more about your rights than your responsibilities, what can you do to change your attitude?

Tom Robbins said, "Don't let yourself be victimized by the age you live in. It's not the times that will bring us down, any more than it's society. There's a tendency today to absolve individuals of moral responsibility and treat them as victims of social circumstance. You buy that and you pay with your soul. What limits people is lack of character." When the character of leaders is low, so are their standards.

What kind of standards do you have? Every leader has certain expectations for himself as well as for his organization. You may have never written them down. Take time now to list the standards that you maintain for yourself and for your organization. What in your life is non-negotiable?

Yourself   **Your Organization**
Example: *Honest Relationships*   *Honesty with the public*

Your character will influence all of the people in your organization. If you maintain high standards, your organization will follow your example.

APPLYING WHAT I'VE LEARNED

People notice more than you think they do, and if you compromise your integrity they will find out. From the standards you listed above (and keeping in mind that your actions influence others) write a personal statement of ethics.

Example: *By maintaining an honest work ethic I will ensure that my actions will not bring disgrace to my organization or myself.*

Day 3
What We Really Are

Let's begin today by doing a little self-examination. In the first section, write down how you think people perceive you. What kind of person do most people think you are? In the second section, write down how you think you really are. What kind of person are you really?

People think I am

I think I really am

Our tendency is to work harder on our image than on our integrity. Image is what people think we are. Integrity is what we really are.

Two older women were walking around a somewhat overcrowded English country churchyard and came upon a tombstone. The inscription said: "Here lies John Smith, a politician and an honest man."

"Good heavens!" said one woman to the other. "Isn't it awful that they had to put two people in the same grave!"

All of us have known those who were not the same on the outside as they were inside. Many who have worked harder on their images than on their integrity don't understand why they suddenly "fall." Even friends who thought they knew them are surprised.

INTEGRITY RESULTS IN A SOLID REPUTATION, NOT JUST AN IMAGE

Thomas Macauley said, "The measure of a man's real character is what he would do if he would never be found out." Life is like a vise; at times it will squeeze us. At those moments of pressure, whatever is inside will be found out. We cannot give what we do not have. Image promises much but produces little. Integrity never disappoints.

Use these questions to determine when you are image-building instead of integrity-building. Answer with yes or no.

Consistency: Are you the same person no matter who you are with? _____

Choices: Do you make decisions based on what is best for others even when another choice would make you look better? _____

Credit: Are you quick to recognize others for their efforts and contributions to your success? _____

If you answered no to any of the above questions, analyze your motives. You may be looking for ways to benefit yourself instead of ways to build your integrity.

In ancient China the people wanted security against the barbaric hordes to the north, so they built the Great Wall. It was so high that no one could climb over it and so thick that nothing could break it down. They settled back to enjoy their security. But during the first hundred years of the wall's existence, China was invaded three times. Not once did the barbaric hordes break down the wall or climb over it. Each time they bribed a gatekeeper and then marched right through the gates. The

Chinese were so busy relying on the strength of their walls of stone that they forgot to teach strength of character to their children.

APPLYING WHAT I'VE LEARNED

Have you discovered a gap between who you are and who others think you are? You can start making choices today that will narrow that gap. List some steps you will take to improve the consistency, choices, or credit in your leadership. Ask a trusted friend or colleague to monitor your progress.

1. _____

2. _____

3. _____

I will ask _____ to keep me accountable.

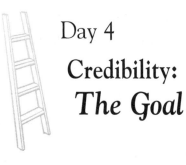

Day 4

Credibility:
The Goal

INTEGRITY MEANS LIVING IT MYSELF
BEFORE LEADING OTHERS

We cannot lead anyone else farther than we have been. Too many times we are so concerned about the product that we try to shortcut the process. There are no short-cuts when integrity is involved. Eventually the truth will come out.

I heard of a man who interviewed a consultant to some of the largest U.S. companies about their quality control. The consultant said, "In quality control, we are not concerned about the product. We are concerned about the process. If the process is right, the product is guaranteed." The same holds true for integrity; it guarantees credibility.

My basketball coach, Don Neff, repeatedly emphasized to our team, "You play like you practice." When we fail to follow this principle, we fail to reach our personal potential. When leaders fail to follow this principle, eventually they lose their credibility.

We can practice integrity in many ways. From being honest in our opinions to not telling people everything that they want to hear, we can put into practice what we are teaching our subordinates. List several ways that you practice integrity:

Words   Actions

INTEGRITY HELPS A LEADER BE CREDIBLE, NOT JUST CLEVER

Fred Smith once shared with me the difference between being clever and being credible: He said that clever leaders never last.

That statement reminded me of the words of Peter Drucker, given to pastors gathered to discuss important issues in the church: "The final requirement of effective leadership is to earn trust. Otherwise there won't be any followers. And the only definition of a leader is someone who has followers. To trust a leader, it is *not* necessary to agree with him. Trust is the conviction that the leader means what he says. It is a belief in something very old-fashioned called 'integrity.' A leader's actions and a leader's professed beliefs must be congruent or at least compatible. Effective leadership—and again this is very old wisdom—is not based on being clever; it is based primarily on being consistent."[3]

How consistent are you? Do you really believe in the ideas you express, or are you just being clever? It is easy to say that cheaters never win, but are you consistently honest in your daily actions? It takes work to be consistent . . . it's an everyday task.

Leaders who are sincere don't have to advertise the fact. It's visible in everything they do and soon becomes common knowledge to everyone. Likewise, insincerity cannot be hidden, disguised, or covered up, no matter how competent a manager may otherwise be.

The only way to keep the goodwill and high esteem of the people you work with is to deserve it. No one can fool all of the people all of the time. Each of us, eventually, is recognized for exactly what we are—not what we try to appear to be.

Ann Landers said, "People of integrity expect to be believed. They also know time will prove them right and are willing to wait." Integrity is lasting.

APPLYING WHAT I'VE LEARNED

Ask someone who knows you well what areas of your life he sees as consistent (you do what you say) and what areas he sees as inconsistent (you say but don't always live). In the following spaces, write down several specific areas in which you feel you could improve. In the second column, think of and write down ways you can improve your integrity in these areas.

Areas That Need Improvement   **Ways to Improve**

Day 5

The Good Fight

INTEGRITY IS A HARD-WON ACHIEVEMENT.

Integrity is not a given factor in everyone's life. It is a result of self-discipline, inner trust, and a decision to be relentlessly honest in all situations. Unfortunately, in today's world of quick fixes, strength of character is a rare commodity. As a result, we have few contemporary models of integrity. Our present culture has produced few enduring heroes, few models of virtue. We have become a nation of imitators, but there are few leaders worth imitating.

List a few contemporary values of our society that don't reflect integrity:

Example: *It's ok to cheat as long as you win.*

The meaning of integrity has been eroded. Drop the word into conversations in Hollywood, on Wall Street, even on Main Street, and you'll get blank stares in return. For most Americans the word conjures up ideas of prudishness or narrow-mindedness. In an age when the meanings of words are manipulated, foundational values such as integrity can be pulverized overnight.

What are we afraid of? Complete the following sentence:

If I practice integrity, most people will think I

This is where the difficulty lies. To practice integrity, we often must go against what society deems reasonable. Integrity is antithetical to the spirit of our age. The overarching philosophy of life that guides our culture revolves around a materialistic, consumer mentality. The craving or need of the moment supersedes consideration of values that have eternal significance.

Billy Graham said, "Integrity is the glue that holds our way of life together. We must constantly strive to keep our integrity intact. When wealth is lost, nothing is lost; when health is lost, something is lost; when character is lost, all is lost."[4]

APPLYING WHAT I'VE LEARNED

As we end this week, look back at the poem by Edgar Guest. Ask yourself these questions:

- *Am I true to myself?* Do I practice what I preach? Do I maintain high standards in myself as well as in those I lead?

- *Am I true to my leader?* Joseph Bailey interviewed more than thirty top executives. He found that all had learned firsthand from a mentor.[5] Ralph Waldo Emerson said, "Our chief want in life is somebody who shall make us what we can be." When we find that person, we need to check our growth on a regular basis, asking, "Am I totally availing myself of the teaching I am receiving?" Taking shortcuts in this process will hurt both your mentor and you.

- *Am I true to my followers?* As leaders, we understand that any wrong decision has an adverse effect on not only us, but also those who follow us. However, making a bad decision because of wrong motives increases the negative effect. Before reaching for the reins of leadership, we must realize that we teach what we know and reproduce what we are.

INTEGRITY IS AN INSIDE JOB

Advocates of leadership, James Kouzes and Barry Posner, report in their book *The Leadership Challenge* that followers expect four things from their leaders[6]:

1. Honesty

2. Competence

3. Vision

4. Inspiration

It's report card time. Give yourself a grade for each area, and next to the grade write a short comment about why you received that grade:

Characteristic	Grade	Comment
Honesty		
Competence		
Vision		
Inspiration		

Which area received the lowest score? How can you work on improving your score?

INTEGRITY
DISCUSSION QUESTIONS

1. It can be said that integrity comprise two components: Knowing your values, and following through on those values. If that is the case, which do you find to be more difficult: Knowing what you believe or following through? Why?

2. When it comes to your values for personal integrity, how do you determine what they are? Where do you look for those standards?

3. Integrity is sometimes defined as having your words and actions match. Do you think people whose actions and words don't match pay a personal cost? If your answer is yes, explain.

4. If reputation is what others think of a person but character is who he or she really is, then which do you think people are most concerned about in our society? In your neighborhood? In your organization?

5. How can a leader regain trust with his followers after he or she has been a poor integrity model?

6. For many people, it's easy to maintain integrity in the big things. They would never engage in theft, character assassination, or fraud, but they have a hard time in the smaller things. Yet for leaders, followers watch everything they do. What little things do you have difficulty with?

7. How can a person help himself or herself to be more consistent in all things—both great and small? Discuss some ways to get on track.

8. The people closest to you know you the best and are therefore in the best position to discern your consistency as an employer, leader, spouse, parent, or child. If you asked the various people in your life how you are doing in the area of integrity, how do you think they would respond?
   A) You live by the highest standards, and you do what you say and say what you do.
   B) You are consistent most of the time and easily engender trust.
   C) You could stand to become more consistent in words and deeds.
   D) You are a mystery—people rarely know what you believe or how you will act.

Week 4

The Ultimate Test of Leadership: *Creating Positive Change*

INTRODUCTION

Change the leader, change the organization. I've said this hundreds of times when conducting leadership conferences. Everything rises and falls on leadership! However, I have found that it's not easy to change leaders. In fact, I've discovered that *leaders resist change as much as followers do*. The result? Unchanged leaders equal unchanged organizations.

PROFILE OF A LEADER IN TROUBLE

Notice that five of the following twelve trouble spots for a leader deal with an unwillingness to change. That spells trouble for the organization.

A leader in trouble . . .

- Has a poor understanding of people.

- Lacks imagination.

- Has personal problems.

- Passes the buck.

- Feels secure and satisfied.

- Is not organized.

- Flies into rages.

- Will not take a risk.

- Is insecure and defensive.

- Stays inflexible.

- Has no team spirit.

- Fights change.

Do you identify with any of the above statements that apply to change? You may need to ask a trusted coworker to review the list with you. If you do find that you are resistant to change or risk-taking and feel insecure when change arises in your organization, start to ask yourself why. Write out any thoughts next to the phrase you identified with. On day two we will go in-depth about why people resist change, and you will want to refer to this list.

The first order of things to be changed is me, the leader. After I consider how hard it is to change myself, then I will understand the challenge of trying to change others. This is the ultimate test of leadership.

A Middle Eastern mystic said, "I was a revolutionary when I was young and all my prayer to God was: 'Lord, give me the energy to change the world.' As I approached middle age and realized that my life was half gone without my changing a single soul, I changed my prayer to: 'Lord, give me the grace to change all those who come into contact with me, just my family and friends, and I shall be satisfied.' Now that I am an old man and my days are numbered, I have begun to see how foolish I have been. My one prayer now is: 'Lord, give me the grace to change myself.' If I had prayed for this right from the start, I would not have wasted my life."[1]

Let's begin this week by answering some of the following questions from Howard Hendricks' book *Teaching to Change Lives*. After each question, write your answer.

Am I growing?

- How have you changed lately? In the last week? (Be specific!)

- The last month?

- The last year?

- Are any of these answers too vague? Why?

- Name one specific way you've been growing recently.

Effective teaching comes only through a changed person. The more you change, the more you become an instrument of change in the lives of others. If you want to become a change agent, you also must change. [2]

A first step in improving your leadership skills is a personal growth plan. If you do not already have one, get started with this exercise. Think of books, tapes, other resources, and conferences that you could use to improve your leadership skills. Make a list of those resources below, and commit yourself to learning in order to improve. Set goals:

I will read _____(number) books this year. (List titles.)

Titles:_____

I will attend the following conference this year: _____

I will take a class on_____

Businessman William A. Hewitt said, "To be a leader you must preserve all through your life the attitude of being receptive to new ideas. The quality of leadership you will give will depend upon your ability to evaluate new ideas, to separate change for the sake of change from change for the sake of men."

This week we will begin to understand how an effective leader must be able to deal with change and anticipate how to make change beneficial. We will examine the following:

- The leader as change agent

- Why people resist change

- The evolutionary process of change

- Creating a climate for change

- Why change will happen

Day 1

The Leader as Change Agent

Once the leader has personally changed and discerned the difference between novel change and needed change, that leader must become a change agent. In this world of rapid change and discontinuities, the leader must be out in front to encourage change and growth and to show the way to bring them about. He must first understand the two important requisites to bringing about change: (1) knowing the technical requirements of the change, and (2) understanding the attitude and motivational demands for bringing it about.

Both requisites are critically necessary. More often than not, though, when failure to change results, it is because of inadequate or inappropriate motivation, not from lack of technical smarts.

A manager usually will be more skilled in the technical requirements of change, whereas the leader will have a better understanding of the attitudinal and motivational demands that the followers need. Note the difference: In the beginning, the skills of a leader are essential. No change will ever occur if the psychological needs are unmet. Once change has begun, the skills of a manager are needed to maintain needed change.

Where are you weaker? Think about a recent change that you initiated with your people. List the instances where the change was resisted or where the change was halted.

Were these roadblocks more motivational or technical?

Motivation problems can reflect a poor understanding of your team's attitude.

You need to focus on learning to read your people. Technical problems can reflect a lack of planning. Your focus should be on discovering and listing all the logistical requirements for the change to succeed.

A good exercise when you face change is to make a list of the logical advantages and disadvantages that should result from the change, and then make another list indicating the psychological impact. Just seeing this on a sheet of paper can be clarifying. You may find yourself saying, "I don't like to admit it, but I'm insecure at this point, even though the change makes sense logically."

Another possibility is that a change you are considering may not affect your psychological security, yet it doesn't make sense logically when you examine the advantages and disadvantages. The key is to distinguish between the logical and the psychological aspects of any change.

Try this exercise on a real-life upcoming change. In the spaces provided, write down the advantages and disadvantages of this change. Try to determine whether the change will bring more positive or negative results. Then note whether the items on each list are logical or psychological.

The Change:

Advantages   Disadvantages

HISTORICAL ACCOUNT OF RESISTANCE TO CHANGE

Resistance to change is universal. It invades all classes and cultures. It seizes every generation by the throat and attempts to stop all forward progress. Many well-educated people, after being confronted with truth, have still been unwilling to change their minds.

For example, for centuries people believed that Aristotle was right when he said that the heavier an object, the faster it would fall to earth. Aristotle was regarded as the greatest thinker of all time, and surely he could not be wrong. All it would have taken was for one brave person to take two objects, one heavy and one light, and drop them from a great height to see whether or not the heavier object landed first. But no one stepped forward until nearly two thousand years after Aristotle's death. In 1589, Galileo summoned learned professors to the base of the Leaning Tower of Pisa. Then he went to the top and pushed off two weights, one weighing ten pounds and the other weighing one pound. Both landed at the same time. But the power of belief in the conventional wisdom was so strong, the professors denied what they had seen. They continued to say Aristotle was right.

With his telescope, Galileo proved the theory of Copernicus, that the earth was not the center of the universe; the earth and the planets revolve around the sun. Yet when he tried to change people's beliefs, he was thrown into prison and spent the rest of his life under house arrest.

APPLYING WHAT I'VE LEARNED

Many people resist change because they would rather hold onto something familiar. This "Attitude" exercise will help you to understand how change is often perceived.

HOW DO YOU WRITE THE WORD ATTITUDE?

Directions: Write the word attitude on the first line with your normal "writing" hand, then on the second line with your other hand.

_____

_____

Application: When you look at the word *attitude* written by the hand you do not normally write with, you see a picture of the kind of attitude we usually have when we are trying to do something new. Someone once said, "Nothing should ever be done for the first time." Every time anyone tries something new, it's a risk. It's usually very difficult and dredges up all kinds of doubts. That's why perseverance is so critical. As you continually practice and work through the change, your attitude will improve. Eventually, your ability to "write with the other hand" will be as good as that with your "normal" hand. With persistence and dedication, you can lead your people through the change.

Day 2

Why People Resist Change

In a "Peanuts" cartoon, Charlie Brown says to Linus: "Perhaps you can give me an answer, Linus. What would you do if you felt that no one liked you?" Linus replies, "I'd try to look at myself objectively, and see what I could do to *improve*. That's *my* answer, Charlie Brown." To which Charlie replies, "I *hate* that answer!" There are a number of reasons why many of us, like Charlie Brown, resist change. Examine each of the following to determine whether it affects you. Check the appropriate box for each.

CHANGE ISN'T SELF-INITIATED

When people lack ownership of an idea, they usually resist it, even when it is in their best interests! They simply don't like the idea of being manipulated or feeling like pawns of the system. Wise leaders allow followers to give input and be a part of the process of change. Most of the time the key to my attitude about change is whether I am initiating it (in which case I am all for it) or someone else is imposing the change on me (which tends to make me more resistant).

Self-evaluation:
- ❏ This affects me.
- ❏ This does not affect me.

ROUTINE IS DISRUPTED

Habits allow us to do things without much thought, which is why most of us have so many of them. Habits are not instincts. They are acquired reactions. They don't just happen; they are caused. First we form habits, but then our habits form us. Change threatens our habit patterns and forces us to think, reevaluate, and sometimes unlearn past behavior.

Self-evaluation:
- ❏ This affects me.
- ❏ This does not affect me.

CHANGE CREATES FEAR OF THE UNKNOWN

Change means traveling in uncharted waters, and this causes our insecurities to rise. Therefore, many people are more comfortable with old problems than with new solutions. Some people are open to change as long as it doesn't inconvenience them or cost anything.

Self-evaluation:
- ❏ This affects me.
- ❏ This does not affect me.

THE PURPOSE OF THE CHANGE IS UNCLEAR

When a decision has been made, the longer it takes for employees to hear and the farther the desired change is from the decision maker, the more resistance it will receive. That's why decisions should be made at the lowest level possible. The decision maker, because of close proximity to the issue, will make a better decision and those most affected by the decision will know it quickly by hearing it from a source close to them and to the problem.

Self-evaluation:
- ❏ This affects me.
- ❏ This does not affect me.

CHANGE CREATES FEAR OF FAILURE

Elbert Hubbard said that the greatest mistake a person can make is to be afraid of making one. It is tragic when success has "gone to my head." It is even more tragic if failure goes to my head. When this happens, I begin to agree with Larry Anderson, who was a pitcher for the San Diego Padres. He said, "If at first you don't succeed, failure may be your thing." Too many people, fearing that failure is their thing, hold tenaciously to whatever they feel comfortable with and continually resist change.

Self-evaluation:
- ❑ This affects me.
- ❑ This does not affect me.

THE REWARDS FOR CHANGE DON'T MATCH THE EFFORT CHANGE REQUIRES

People will not change until they perceive that the advantages of changing outweigh the disadvantages of continuing with the way things are. What leaders sometimes fail to recognize is that the followers will always weigh the advantage/disadvantage issue in light of personal gain/loss, not organizational gain/loss.

Self-evaluation:
- ❑ This affects me.
- ❑ This does not affect me.

THE FOLLOWERS LACK RESPECT FOR THE LEADER

When followers don't like the leader who oversees the change, their feelings won't allow them to look at the change objectively. In other words, people view the change according to the way they view the change agent.

Self-evaluation:
- ❑ This affects me.
- ❑ This does not affect me.

CHANGE MAY MEAN PERSONAL LOSS

Whenever change is imminent, the question on everyone's mind is, "How will this affect me?" Usually there are three groups of people within the organization: (1) those who will lose; (2) those who are neutral; and (3) those who will benefit. Each group is different and must be handled with sensitivity, but also with straightforwardness.

Self-evaluation:
☐ This affects me.
☐ This does not affect me.

CHANGE REQUIRES ADDITIONAL COMMITMENT

Time is the most precious commodity for many people. Whenever change is about to happen, we all look to see how it will affect our time. Usually we conclude that change will be fine *if* it does not increase our time commitment. Sidney Howard said that one half of knowing what you want is knowing what you must give up before you get it. When the cost of change is time, many will resist the change.

Self-evaluation:
☐ This affects me.
☐ This does not affect me.

APPLYING WHAT I'VE LEARNED

As you encounter the need to make changes, be aware of what resistance you may encounter, either from yourself or from others.

THINKING AHEAD:

What fears stand in the way of you or your team? Measure the fears against the possibilities:

Benefits of the Change
(facing fear)

Benefits of Avoiding Change
(not facing fear)

PRESENTING THE IDEA:

How does your team respond to new ideas? Would they react better if they heard the announcement from someone else? If so, who? How can you arrange for this to happen?

List ways you can give your team members ownership of an idea. (Day 5 will give you more details about ownership.)

SEEING THE CHANGE THROUGH:

How can you help your team keep their focus on the benefits of the change even in times of discouragement?

By understanding how your team will respond to change and by preparing for the questions that follow, you will become a more effective change agent.

Day 3

The Evolution of Change

People change when they *hurt* enough that they *have* to change; *learn* enough that they *want* to change; or *receive* enough that they are *able* to change. The leader must recognize when people are in one of these three stages. In fact, top leaders create an atmosphere that causes one of these three things to occur.[2]

It is helpful to remember that change can be seen as either *revolutionary* (something totally different from what has been) or *evolutionary* (a refinement of what has been). It is usually easier to present change as a simple refinement of "the way we've been doing it" rather than something big, new, and completely different.

When a proposal for change is introduced in the organization, people fall into five categories in terms of their response:

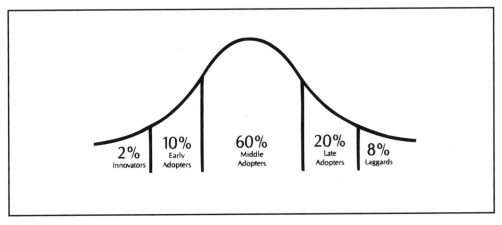

1. **Innovators are the dreamers.** They are the originators of new ideas and generally are not acknowledged as leaders or policy makers.

2. **Early adopters are those who know a good idea when they see it.** Their opinions are respected in the organization. Although they did not create the idea, they will try to convince others to accept it.

3. **Middle adopters are the majority.** They will respond to the opinions of others. Generally they are reasonable in their analysis of a new idea, but inclined to maintain the status quo. They can be influenced by the positive or negative influencers of the organization.

4. **Late adopters are the last group to endorse an idea.** They often speak against proposed changes and may never verbally acknowledge acceptance. Generally they will adopt it if the majority demonstrates support.

5. **Laggards are always against change.** Their commitment is to the status quo and the past. Often they try to create division within the organization.

   In general, which group would you be in?_____

List some of your top team members and which group they're usually in?

Most teams have a mix of the five different groups. But by approaching your people in order, as you introduce change, you can rally them and create the momentum that carries the later adopters.

This is the evolutionary process of successful change within an organization.

The Stages of Change

Step 1: **Ignorance.** No unified direction or sense of priorities is felt among the followers. They are "in the dark."

Step 2: **Information.** General information is given to the people. Initially the ideas for change are not embraced.

Step 3: **Infusion.** The penetration of new ideas into the status quo may cause confrontations with apathy, prejudice, and tradition. The general tendency is to focus on problems.

Step 4: **Individual Change.** The "early adopters" begin to see the benefits of the proposed change and embrace them. Personal convictions replace complacency.

Step 5: **Organizational Change.** Two sides of the issue are being discussed. Less defensiveness and more openness concerning proposed changes can be observed. The momentum shifts from anti-change to pro-change.

Step 6: **Awkward Application.** Some failures and some successes are experienced as the change is implemented. The learning process is rapid.

Step 7: **Integration.** Awkwardness begins to decrease and the acceptance level increases. A growing sense of accomplishment and a secondary wave of results and successes occur.

Step 8: **Innovation.** Significant results create confidence and a willingness to take risks. The result is a willingness to change more rapidly and boldly.

As Step 8 is taken, the organization as a whole is more willing to go through the process again. The major effect of the process develops as the majority of the organization is exposed repeatedly to the new idea.

APPLYING WHAT I'VE LEARNED

Take some time today to chart a recent change that occurred under your leadership. Make notes on how your team experienced each step.

Step 1: Ignorance _____

Step 2: Information _____

Step 3: Infusion _____

Step 4: Individual Change _____

Step 5: Organizational Change _____

Step 6: Awkward Application _____

Step 7: Integration _____

Step 8: Innovation _____

Here are some question to answer: What step did you start on? Did you skip any steps? What step did you stay on the longest?

The next time a new idea is introduced to you and your team, be prepared. By knowing where you will have to start and what step you will be on the longest, you will understand the process and hopefully help your team to avoid frustrations. For example, if your team gets hung up on Step 3, be prepared to point out the positive effects of the change and the benefits of the change to your team.

Day 4

Creating a Climate for Change

Human behavior studies show that people do not basically resist change; they resist "being changed." But unless the people themselves are changed, no other change will happen. The first statement this week read, "Change the leader, change the organization." Now we will start with the leader and develop a strategy for the organization. To create a climate for change . . .

THE LEADER MUST DEVELOP
A TRUST WITH PEOPLE

It is wonderful when the people believe in the leader. It is more wonderful when the leader believes in the people. When both are a reality, trust is the result. The more people trust the leader, the more willing they will be to accept the leader's proposed changes.

My first question to a leader who wants to make changes within an organization is always, "What is your relationship with your people?" If the relationship is positive, then the leader is ready to take the next step.

How would you answer that question? What steps have you taken since last week to improve your level of trust?

THE LEADER MUST MAKE PERSONAL CHANGES BEFORE ASKING OTHERS TO CHANGE

As we have already discussed, *your* attitude toward change will greatly affect the way your workers accept change. It is not enough to say you are going to change. You must take action. Andrew Carnegie said, "As I grow older, I pay less attention to what men say. I just watch what they do." We have gone over it before: Your followers are watching you, and if you won't change, why should they?

GOOD LEADERS UNDERSTAND THE HISTORY OF THE ORGANIZATION

Previously we went over the importance of knowing the history of your organization in order to become more of a team player and rally your followers. Knowing the history of your organization can also help you know how to present ideas and changes. The longer an organization has gone without change, the more effort introducing it will require. Also, when change is implemented and the result is negative, people within the organization will be leery of embracing future changes. The opposite is also true. Successful changes in the past prepare people to readily accept more changes.

PLACE INFLUENCERS IN LEADERSHIP POSITIONS, AND SOLICIT THEIR SUPPORT BEFORE PRESENTING CHANGE TO EVERYONE

Leaders have two characteristics. First, they are going somewhere; and second, they are able to persuade other people to go with them. Complete this list to solicit support for a change from the major influencers in the organization.

1. List the major influencer(s) of the major groups within your organization. (There should be names from your top 20 list here.)

2. Who will be affected directly by the change? (These people are the most important group.)

3. Who will be affected indirectly by this change?

4. Who will probably respond positively?

5. Who will probably respond negatively?

6. Which group is the majority?

7. Which group is the most influential?

•   If the positive group is stronger, bring the influencers together for discussion.

•   If the negative group is stronger, meet with the influencers individually.

8. What do you consider the "key" to each influencer?

ENCOURAGE THE INFLUENCERS TO INFLUENCE OTHERS INFORMALLY

Major changes should not surprise people. A "leadership leak" done properly will prepare the people for the formal meeting.

Each year I explain to my key leaders that they carry two buckets around with them. One bucket is filled with gasoline and the other with water. Whenever there is a "little fire" of contention within the organization because the people fear a possible change, the influencers are the first to hear about it. When they arrive on the scene they will either throw the bucket of gasoline on the situation and really cause a problem, or they will throw the bucket of water on the little fire and extinguish the problem. In other words, key influencers are either the leader's greatest asset or his greatest liability.

Leadership leaks should be planned and positive, preparing the people for the meeting where the change will be formally presented.

APPLYING WHAT I'VE LEARNED

Creating a climate for change is the best way for a leader to facilitate an ever-changing situation. At your next meeting with your "top 20 percent," introduce the concept of the buckets of gasoline and water. Explain how they can defuse hostile situations. Also go over the steps needed for a successful leadership leak. Who should be told? How long before telling the entire organization?

Day 5

Change Will Happen

Within the human condition, there is one certainty—things change. As a leader, you must be willing to accept and anticipate change, and use changes for the benefit of your organization. However, it is not wise to be the one solely responsible for change. The people under your leadership must partner with you in change. If they do not feel connected to the change, the leader will be isolated and reduce his ability to lead.

GIVE THE PEOPLE OWNERSHIP OF THE CHANGE

Openness by the leader paves the way for ownership by the people. Without ownership, changes will be short-term. Here are some ways to help your people own change:

- Inform people in advance so they'll have time to think about the implications of the change and how it will affect them.

- Explain the overall objectives of the change—the reasons for it and how and when it will occur.

- Show people how the change will benefit them. Be honest with the employees who may lose out as a result of the change. Alert them early and provide assistance to help them find another job if necessary.

- Ask those who will be affected by the change to participate in all stages of the change process.

- Keep communication channels open. Provide opportunities for employees to discuss the change. Encourage questions, comments, and other feedback.

- Be flexible and adaptable throughout the change process. Admit mistakes and make changes where appropriate.

- Constantly demonstrate your belief in and commitment to the change. Indicate your confidence in their ability to implement the change.

- Provide enthusiasm, assistance, appreciation, and recognition to those implementing the change.

The question should not be "Will we ever change?" but "When and how much will we change?" Nothing stays the same except the fact that change is always present. Not all change is improvement, but without change there can be no improvement.

Change=Growth
or
Change=Grief

Change represents both possible opportunity and potential loss. My observation is that change becomes grief when:

- The change proposed is a bad idea.

- The change proposed is not accepted by the influencers.

- The change proposed is not presented effectively.

- The change proposed is self-serving to the leaders.

- The change proposed is based solely on the past.

- The changes proposed are too many, too quickly.

APPLYING WHAT I'VE LEARNED

Because change is inevitable, below are the questions you should review *before* attempting changes within an organization. When the questions can be answered with "yes," change tends to be easier. Questions that can be answered with "no" (or "maybe") may be "red flags" that either the change or its timing is not right for your organization.

Yes	No	
____	____	Will this change benefit the followers?
____	____	Is this change compatible with the purpose of the organization?
____	____	Is this change specific and clear?
____	____	Are the top 20 percent (the influencers) in favor of this change?
____	____	Is it possible to test this change before making a total commitment to it?
____	____	Are physical, financial, and human resources available to make this change?
____	____	Is this change reversible?
____	____	Is this change the next obvious step?
____	____	Does this change have both short- and long-range benefits?
____	____	Is the leadership capable of bringing about this change?
____	____	Is the timing right?

Focus on the "no" answers. Are there ways to modify the plans for change so that you can answer "yes?"

CREATING POSITIVE CHANGE
DISCUSSION QUESTIONS

1. This week you read that to change an organization, you must first change the leader. Do you agree with that statement? Why?

2. What kinds of things happen when the leader refuses to change while the rest of the people in the organization want to try new things to improve it?

3. Why do most people resist change?

4. How well do you accept change? The measure is not how boldly you fight to see your own ideas implemented; it's how well you adapt to the ideas of others. In which group do you usually find yourself when others suggest changes that will affect you?
   A) Innovator
   B) Early Adopters
   C) Middle Adopters
   D) Late Adopters
   E) Laggards

5. Think about a big change affecting others that you had to implement some time in the past. Did it require greater technical expertise or people skills? How did you handle it?

6. For people to accept change, they have to own it. How does a leader help people to own his or her vision?

7. If you had to implement an unpopular change in your organization immediately, which of the following would best describe your strategy? Why?
   A) Inform everyone together of the change and expect them to accept it
   B) Personally inform only people in positions of authority and ask them to tell everyone else
   C) Try to personally gain the trust of the influencers in the organization and then ask them to help you as you try to win everyone else to the change
   D) Try personally to win as many people as possible to the change

8. Where does modeling come into play in organizational change?

9. How well are you modeling an attitude of acceptance, integration, and innovation in your organization? How can you improve?

Week 5

The Quickest Way to Gain Leadership:
Problem Solving

INTRODUCTION

According to F. F. Fournies, writing in *Coaching for Improved Work Performance*,[1] there are four common reasons why people do not perform the way they should:

1. They do not know *what* they are supposed to do.

2. They do not know *how* to do it.

3. They do not know *why* they should.

4. There are obstacles beyond their control.

These four reasons why people fail to perform at their potential are all responsibilities of leadership. The first three reasons deal with starting a job correctly. A training program, job description, proper tools, and vision, along with good communication skills, will go a long way in effectively meeting the first three issues.

This week we will deal with the fourth reason why many people fail to reach their performance potential. It's how they deal with problems. Problems continually occur at work, at home, and in life in general. My observation is that people generally dislike problems, weary of them quickly, and will do almost anything to get away

from them. This climate makes others place the reins of leadership into your hands—
if you are willing and able to either tackle their problems or train them to solve their
problems. Your problem-solving skills will always be needed because people will
always have problems.

This week's lesson will deal with the two things needed to effectively solve
problems: (1) the right attitude and (2) the right action plan.

**List just a few problems that you are currently facing, either at home, at
work, or in private:**

They can seem overwhelming, can't they?

We all have problems. But sometimes we think that our generation has more
problems than the last. I was reminded of that when I read the words of Dwight
Bohmbach in *What's Right with America:* "America's elders lived through the great
1929 stock market crash that ruined many of their families; the Depression years; the
Bonus March on Washington, when veterans were dispersed by Army troops; the
New Deal years; Pearl Harbor; the loss of the Philippines; years of long days and
nights in defense plants in the 1940s; fighting in Europe and the Pacific; D-Day; the
Battle of the Bulge; V-E Day; the hope-filled beginning of the United Nations in
America; the A-bomb; V-J Day; the Marshall Plan in Europe; the Berlin airlift; war
in Korea; the U-2 incident; the Bay of Pigs invasion; the Cuban missile crisis; the
killings of President Kennedy, Bobby Kennedy, and Martin Luther King; the civil
rights struggle; the Vietnam War; Americans on the moon; Watergate and the resig-
nation of a president and vice president; the energy crisis; Three-Mile Island; Iranian
hostages; a new president shot in 1981; the bombing of our embassy and hundreds of
Marines in Lebanon; becoming a debtor nation, with the highest budget deficit in
history. What a lifetime!" We should remember the words of Paul Harvey, who said

that in times like these, it is always helpful to remember that there have always been times like these.

This is not to trivialize your problems. Of course they are huge when they are happening to you. This week our goal is to deal with these challenges. We will look at the nature of problems and effective ways of dealing with them as a leader. You will come to understand the following:

- The nature of problems

- The problem-solving leader

- The right attitude—the right action

- The problem-solving process

- Solving and avoiding future problems

As you work this week, remember some important facts:

- The size of the person is more important than the size of the problems.

- People need to change their perspectives, not their problems.

- Always take the "high road" versus the "low road" in seeking solutions.

Day 1

The Nature of Problems

PROBLEMS GIVE MEANING TO LIFE

A wise philosopher once commented that an eagle's only obstacle to overcome for flying with greater speed and ease is the air. Yet if the air were withdrawn, and the proud bird were to fly in a vacuum, it would fall instantly to the ground, unable to fly at all. The very element that offers resistance to flying is at the same time the condition for flight. Likewise, the main obstacle that a powerboat has to overcome is the water against the propeller, yet if it were not for this same resistance, the boat would not move at all.

The same law—that obstacles are conditions of success—holds true in human life. A life free of all obstacles and difficulties would reduce all possibilities and powers to zero. Eliminate problems, and life loses its creative tension. The problem of mass ignorance gives meaning to education. The problem of ill health gives meaning to medicine. The problem of social disorder gives meaning to government.

We all have a tendency to want to get rid of problems and responsibilities. When that temptation arises, remember the youth who was questioning a lonely older man. "What is life's heaviest burden?" he asked. The older fellow answered sadly, "Having nothing to carry."

This positive perspective on problems may be new to you. Do you believe that it's valid? If so, complete the following sentence:

Problems give meaning to my life by

MANY OUTSTANDING PEOPLE HAVE OVER-COME PROBLEMS IN THEIR LIVES

Many of the Psalms were born in difficulty. Gordon MacDonald once said, "Most of the Epistles were written in prisons. Most of the greatest thoughts of the greatest thinkers of all time had to pass through the fire. Bunyan wrote *Pilgrim's Progress* from jail. Florence Nightingale, too ill to move from her bed, reorganized the hospitals of England. Semi-paralyzed and under constant menace of apoplexy, Pasteur was tireless in his attack on disease. During the greater part of his life, American historian Francis Parkman suffered so acutely that he could not work for more than five minutes at a time. His eyesight was so wretched that he could scrawl only a few gigantic words on a manuscript, but he contrived to write twenty magnificent volumes of history."[2]

Bury a person in the snows of Valley Forge, and you have a George Washington. Raise him in abject poverty, and you have an Abraham Lincoln. Strike him down with polio, and he becomes a Franklin D. Roosevelt. Burn him so severely that the doctors say he will never walk again, and you have a Glenn Cunningham, who set the world's one-mile record in 1934. Have him or her born black in a society filled with racial discrimination, and you have a Booker T. Washington, a Marian Anderson, a George Washington Carver, or a Martin Luther King Jr. Call him a slow learner and retarded, and write him off as uneducable, and you have an Albert Einstein.

Because problems exist for everyone, it is necessary to have the ability to overcome them. What are some problems in your life that you have had to overcome?

MY PROBLEM IS NOT MY PROBLEM

There is a world of difference between a person who has a big problem and a person who makes a problem big. For several years I would do between twenty and thirty hours of counseling each week. I soon discovered that the people who came to see me were not necessarily the ones who had the most problems. They were the ones who were problem conscious and found their difficulties stressful. Naive at first, I would try to fix their problems only to discover they would go out and find others.

Their "problems" are not their real problems. The problem is that they react wrongly to "problems" and therefore make their "problems" real problems. What really counts is not what happens *to me* but what happens *in me*.

Think about how you overcame one of the problems you previously listed. If you knew then what you know now, would your reaction be any different? How? How can you continue to learn from your previous reactions?

A study of three hundred highly successful people, people like Franklin Delano Roosevelt, Helen Keller, Winston Churchill, Albert Schweitzer, Mahatma Gandhi, and Albert Einstein, reveals that one-fourth had disabilities, such as blindness, deafness, or the inability to walk. Three-fourths had been born in poverty, came from broken homes, or at least came from exceedingly tense or disturbed situations.

Why did these people overcome problems while thousands are overwhelmed by theirs? They refused to hold on to the common excuses for failure. They turned their stumbling blocks into stepping-stones. They realized they could not determine every circumstance in life, but they could determine their choice of attitude toward every circumstance.

APPLYING WHAT I'VE LEARNED

We all have obstacles, little things that get in the way of our goals. What makes us successful in our journey is our reaction to these obstacles. Think back on the problems you listed in previous answers today. How were they stepping stones to success? Restate them below with this new perspective in mind. What have you learned from them? How can you use this knowledge when you encounter future obstacles?

Stepping Stone   **Lesson Learned**   **How I Apply This to My Jouney**

Day 2

The Problem-Solving Leader

A PROBLEM IS SOMETHING
I CAN DO SOMETHING ABOUT

In 1925, an American company manufacturing and marketing shaving cream was concerned about the effectiveness of its roadside advertising. With the introduction of "high speed" automobiles, the company was concerned that nobody had time to read its billboards. So the company, Burma Shave, created a series of small signs spaced at sufficient intervals so they could be read even at high speeds. The unique approach to advertising made Burma Shave a household name for forty-six years.

As a child growing up in Ohio, I loved the Burma Shave advertisements. This was my favorite:

> A peach looks good
> With lots of fuzz . . .
> But man's no peach . . .
> And never was.

The Burma Shave company became creative in response to a changing society. Be careful in resigning yourself to the position that there is no answer to a problem. Someone else may come along with a solution.

A TEST OF A LEADER IS THE ABILITY TO RECOGNIZE A PROBLEM BEFORE IT BECOMES AN EMERGENCY

Under excellent leadership a problem seldom reaches gigantic proportions because it is recognized and fixed in its early stages.

Great leaders usually recognize a problem in the following sequence:

1. They sense it before they see it (intuition).

2. They begin looking for it and ask questions (curiosity).

3. They gather data (processing).

4. They share their feelings and findings with a few trusted colleagues (communicating).

5. They define the problem (writing).

6. They check their resources (evaluating).

7. They make a decision (leading).

Great leaders are seldom blindsided. They realize that the punch that knocks them out is seldom the hard one—it's the one they didn't see coming. Therefore, they are always looking for signs and indicators that will give them insight into the problem ahead and their odds of fixing it.

Evaluate how you dealt with a recent problem. How many of the steps did you take?

❑ Intuition—Did you sense the problem before it was obvious to others?

❑ Curiosity—What, who, and how did you ask without causing alarm?

❑ Processing—What information did you gather?

❑ Communicating—Who did you share your concerns with?

❑ Writing—How did you define the real problem?

❑ Evaluating—What resources did you already have or need to gather to solve it?

❑ Leading—What decision did you make to solve the problem?

YOU CAN JUDGE LEADERS BY THE SIZE OF THE PROBLEMS THEY TACKLE

In my observation of people and their problems, I have noticed that the size of the person is more important than the size of the problem. Problems look larger or smaller according to whether the person is large or small.

I knew a woman named Marcia who was diagnosed with cancer, had a mastectomy, and completely recovered. In my observation, there seemed to be a big difference between Marcia and others who had the same problem. I almost could have predicted physical recovery for Marcia because she was positive from the beginning of her problem. She handled her problem in a "big" way. Your focus as a leader should be to build big people, because big people will handle big issues effectively.

SOLVE TASK PROBLEMS QUICKLY; PEOPLE PROBLEMS WILL TAKE LONGER

Solving problems may be the immediate agenda, but that should never be where we spend most of our time. If all we do is focus on solving the next problem at hand, we will soon feel like the farmer who said, "The hardest thing about milking cows is that they never stay milked." Problems never stop, but people can stop problems. My suggestions for producing problem solvers are:

1. Make a time commitment to people. Those who never take time to develop people are forced to take time to solve their problems.

2. Never solve a problem for a person; solve it with that person. Take that individual through the sequence that has already been given for recognizing a problem.

APPLYING WHAT I'VE LEARNED

Problems should be solved at the lowest level possible. President John F. Kennedy said that President Eisenhower gave him this advice the day before his inauguration: "You'll find no easy problems ever come to the President of the United States. If they are easy to solve, somebody else has solved them." That statement should be true of every leader. Climbing the ladder of leadership means that fewer but more important decisions will be made.

Make a list of specific ways you can enable your people to solve the problems they can on their own. (Examples: training and empowerment)

Day 3

The Right Attitude—The Right Action

THE RIGHT ATTITUDE

Norman Vincent Peale was right when he said that positive thinking is how you *think* about a problem. Enthusiasm is how you *feel* about a problem. The two together determine what you *do* about a problem. If I could do anything for people, I would help them change their perspectives, not their problems. Positive thinking does not always change our circumstances, but it will always change us. When we are able to think right about tough situations, then our journeys through life become better.

Do you consider yourself to be a positive thinker? Why?

G. W. Target, in his essay "The Window," tells the story of two men confined to hospital beds in the same room. Both men were seriously ill and though they were not allowed much diversion—no television, radio, or books—their friendship developed over months of conversation. They discussed every possible subject in which they both had interest or experience, from family to jobs to vacations, as well as much of their own personal histories.

Neither man left his bed, but one was fortunate enough to be next to the window. As part of his treatment he could sit up in bed for just an hour a day. At this time he would describe the world outside to his roommate. In very descriptive terms he would bring the outside world inside to this friend, describing to him the beautiful park he could see, with its lake, and the many interesting people he saw spending their time there. His friend began to live for those descriptions.

After a particularly fascinating report, the one man began to think it was not fair that his friend got to see everything while he could see nothing. He was ashamed of his thoughts, but he had quite a bit of time to think and he couldn't get this out of his mind. Eventually his thoughts began to take their effect on his health, and he became even more ill, with a disposition to match.

One evening his friend, who sometimes had difficulty with congestion and breathing, awoke with a fit of coughing and choking and was unable to push the button for the nurse to come to his aid. The frustrated, sour man lay there looking at the ceiling, listening to this struggle for life next to him, and doing nothing. The next morning the day nurse came in to find the man by the window dead.

After a proper interval, the man who was so eager to see out that window asked if he could be moved, and it was quickly done. As soon as the room was empty, the man struggled up on his elbow to look out the window and fill his spirit with the sights of the outside world. It was then he discovered the window faced a blank wall.[3]

This story shows how our positive outlook doesn't only benefit us but others as well. How does your outlook benefit others? Are you more like the man describing the beautiful world outside, or the man who is jealous of the view?

THE RIGHT ACTION PLAN

Isn't it true that too many times we have a surplus of simple answers and a shortage of simple problems? Occasionally we all feel like the guy in a cartoon who said, "I try to take just one day at a time, but lately several days have attacked me at once." One thing is certain: Life is not problem-free!

Some people assume that a foolproof plan can be developed for their lives. Others assume that something will go wrong and they will need a backup system. Too many times when a problem arises, we want to blame someone else and take the easy way out.

APPLYING WHAT I'VE LEARNED

Having the right attitude and action plan is essential to dealing with problems. As you work this week, use the space provided to document several problems, your attitude toward each problem, and the action that you took or will take to resolve the problem. You should be able to see how your attitude and action affect your leadership.

Problem 1:

My Attitude:

My Action:

Problem 2:

My Attitude:

My Action:

Problem 3:

My Attitude:

My Action:

Problem 4:

My Attitude:

My Action:

Problem 5:

My Attitude:

My Action:

Day 4
The Problem-Solving Process

Now, even if we don't wish to duck responsibilities and we have a right attitude and a solid action plan, it is still important to follow a process when we're looking for a solution. I suggest following these three steps to problem solving.

IDENTIFY THE PROBLEM

Too many times we attack the symptoms, not the cause. Ordering your staff to stay at their desks until quitting time is a Band-Aid solution that does not answer the question, "Why do they leave early?" *Your job is to identify the real issues that lie beneath the symptoms.*

PRIORITIZE THE PROBLEM

Richard Sloma says to never try to solve all the problems all at once—make them line up for you one-by-one. Whether you face three problems, thirty, or three hundred, "make them stand in single file so you face only one at a time." Approach these problems, not with a view of finding what you hope will be there, but to get the truth and the realities that must be grappled with. You may not like what you find. In that case, you are entitled to try to change it. But do not deceive yourself. What you do find may or may not be the real problem.

DEFINE THE PROBLEM

In a single sentence, answer the question, "What is the problem?" Bobb Biehl encourages us to keep in mind the difference between solving a problem and making a decision. A "decision is a choice you make between two or more alternatives, such as 'Should I fly to Phoenix or Chicago?' A problem is a situation that's counter to your intentions or expectations: 'I meant to fly to Chicago, but I ended up in Detroit,' or 'I meant to have $50,000 in the bank, but I'm $50,000 in the hole.'"[4]

Defining the problem in a single sentence is a four-step process.

1. Ask the right questions.

If you have a vague idea, don't ask a general question such as "What is happening here?" and don't speculate. Instead, ask process-related questions. Two words that always govern my questions are *trends* and *timing*. Most problem trails can be sniffed out if specific questions are asked in these two areas.

2. Talk to the right people.

Beware of authorities with a we-know-better attitude. These people have blind spots and are resistant to change. Creativity is essential for problem solving.

3. Get the hard facts.

Remember Peter Drucker's words, "Once the facts are clear, the decisions jump out at you." Don't let someone say to you, "That person is a good worker." Get concrete examples of that individual's performance. Listen to what is *not* being said and gather the important data.

4. Get involved in the process.

Most problems are not what they seem. Don't just ask the right questions and gather hard facts. Get involved in the process by doing the actual jobs of the people concerned and see what problems arise. Problems should be solved at the lowest level possible because that is where they appear. That is also the level where they are most clearly defined.

APPLYING WHAT I'VE LEARNED

Use the problem-solving process for a current problem you are facing:

Identify the problem:

Prioritize the problem (High Importance/High Urgency, etc.):

Define the problem (in a single sentence):

Day 5

Solving and Avoiding Future Problems

Once you have identified, prioritized, and defined the problem you are dealing with, you are able to apply solutions that will not only solve the current problem, but will also help you keep the same problem from recurring. Keep a current problem in mind when going through today's lesson. Fill in the blanks based on this problem.

SELECT PEOPLE TO HELP YOU IN THE PROBLEM-SOLVING PROCESS

John K. Clemens wrote about Socrates, a very effective problem solver, "Socrates developed this method 2,400 years ago: After defining the problem at hand, he would gather others around him and ask for their opinions and logical support to back their opinions up. As self-appointed gadfly, Socrates spent most of his life causing trouble in complacent, conservative Athens. By debating, cajoling, and prodding, he forced Athenians to question beliefs they took for granted. This finally got him into trouble. The Athenians charged him with impiety toward the gods and corrupting Athens' youth. He was thrown into prison, tried, and sentenced to death. After a month, during which he refused friends' offers to help him escape, Socrates drank a cup of hemlock and died. Nobody expects you to go that far. But practicing the Socratic method will help you be a better leader."[5]

Before inviting people to attend a problem-solving meeting, ask these questions:

- Is it a real problem?

- Is it urgent?

- Is the true nature of the problem known?

- Is it specific? (If the people talk about everything, they will eventually talk about nothing.)

- Has the group most competent to discuss the problem been informed of the problem, and is each participant concerned about solving this issue?

COLLECT PROBLEM CAUSES

List all the possible causes of the problem by asking what caused the problem and how the problem can be avoided in the future.

Causes of the problem:

Ways to avoid the problem:

COLLECT PROBLEM-SOLVING SOLUTIONS

List as many solutions to a problem as possible. The more, the better. Seldom is there just one way to solve a problem. Options are essential because a problem continually shifts and changes. The leader without a backup solution for the primary answer will soon be in trouble.

Possible solutions:

PRIORITIZE AND SELECT THE "BEST" SOLUTIONS

Weigh all the possible solutions before deciding. The leader should always ask the following questions:

- Which solution has the greatest potential to be right?

- Which solution is in the best interests of the organization?

- Which solution has momentum and timing on its side?

- Which solution has the greatest chance for success?

IMPLEMENT THE BEST SOLUTION

Norman Bushnell, founder of Atari, said, "Everyone who's ever taken a shower has an idea. It's the person who gets out of the shower, dries off, and does something about it, who makes a difference."

EVALUATE THE SOLUTION

Let others test out and punch holes in your solution. If they punch intellectual holes (such as, "I don't think it will continue working because . . ."), ignore them. If they point out real operative problems you can observe, then you must make the adjustments. Ask these questions to evaluate the responses:

- Were we able to identify the real causes of the problem?

- Did we make the right decision?

- Has the problem been resolved?

- Have the key people accepted this solution?

- Did I help people to develop problem-solving skills to manage conflict in the future?

APPLYING WHAT I'VE LEARNED

It's important to remember that if you are always the problem solver and never teach the people around you to think and decide for themselves, you will have a dependent group of followers. Many years ago I decided to focus on helping people solve problems rather than helping solve people's problems.

Use these guidelines when you approach your next problem as a team:

- **Never allow others to think you always have the best answers.** This will only make them dependent on you.

- **Ask questions.** Help people to think through the entire process of their problem.

- **Become a coach, not a king.** A coach brings out the best in others, helping them to reach deep down inside and discover their potential. A king only gives commands.

- **List their solutions on paper.** Integrate your ideas with theirs until they have ownership of them.

- **Ask them to decide on the best solution to their problem.**

- **Develop a game plan.**

- **Ask them to take ownership and responsibility for the game plan.** Let them set up a time frame and accountability process.

When the meeting is over, your team members should have processed the problem, selected a solution, developed a game plan, and taken ownership of it. Their relationship with you will not be dependent, but rather deepening.

PROBLEM SOLVING
DISCUSSION QUESTIONS

1. If your problem is not your problem, as you read this week, then how would you define a "real" problem?

2. One of the ironies of life is that a person's strength is also the source of his or her weakness. For example, tenacity, which is positive, sometimes turns into bullying. Patience can turn into sloth. Intelligence can become arrogance. What strength do you possess that sometimes becomes the source of personal problems?

3. Why do you think people problems take so much longer than problem solving that involves just tasks?

4. This week you read that people often experience performance difficulties for three reasons: a) They don't know what they are supposed to do, b) They don't know how they are supposed to do it, or c) They don't know why they are supposed to do what they should do. As a leader, which have you found to be the greatest problem for your people?

5. How can you improve as a communicator to make things easier for your people?

6. One of the signs that leaders are in trouble is that they see problems later than their followers do. Have you ever been part of an organization where you saw a leader get blindsided because he or she didn't see the problems? If so, explain what happened. Is there anything the person could have done to avoid it?

7. If the way people think and feel about a problem impacts how (or whether) they solve it, then how can you create an environment in your organization where people approach problems positively?

8. If you can measure leaders by the size of the problems they tackle, what does that say about you? What kind of problems are you solving?

Week 6

The Extra Plus in Leadership:
Attitude

INTRODUCTION

When I speak at a leadership conference, I often ask everyone to do this exercise:

Write the name of a friend whom you greatly admire:

Write one thing that you admire most about that friend:

Take a moment and do this exercise before you continue reading. I think you'll gain an interesting and important insight. After all the conference participants have completed this exercise, I ask them to tell me their answers. I list the first twenty-five responses on an overhead projector for everyone to see. I put an *A* beside the characteristics that describe attitudes, an *S* beside those describing skills, and an *L* if the words deal with looks. Every time I conduct this exercise, 95 percent of the descriptive words represent attitudes for which the friends are admired.

What does attitude mean to you? Briefly define attitude in your own words.

Attitude is

Chuck Swindoll said, "The longer I live, the more I realize the impact of attitude on life. Attitude, to me, is more important than facts. It is more important than the past, than education, than money, than circumstances, than failures, than successes, than what other people think or say or do. It is more important than appearance, giftedness, or skill. It will make or break a company, a church, or a home. The remarkable thing is that we have a choice every day regarding the attitude we will embrace for that day. We cannot change our past. Nor can we change the fact that people will act in a certain way. We also cannot change the inevitable. The only thing that we can do is play on the one string we have, and that is our attitude. I am convinced that life is 10 percent what happens to me and 90 percent how I react to it. And so it is with you—we are in charge of our attitudes."[1]

Just as our attitudes are the extra pluses in life, they also make the difference in leading others. Leadership has less to do with position than it does with disposition. The disposition of a leader is important because it will influence the way the followers think and feel. Great leaders understand that the right attitude will set the right atmosphere that enables the right responses from others.

What is your disposition? Briefly describe how you feel about each of the following areas:

Your position at work: _____

Your salary at work: _____

The time you spend working: _____

Your work responsibilities: _____

Your coworkers: _____

Those in leadership over you: _____

THIS WEEK AS WE FOCUS ON ATTITUDE, WE WILL LEARN ABOUT:

- Your attitude: your most important asset

- The bad attitude

- A leader's attitude

- How to change your attitude

- A new attitude

Before you begin this week, take a few minutes to reflect on your attitude toward life. How do you feel about the things you are involved with? In the following space, make a short journal entry describing your opinions and feelings about your life right now. Often, it is not what is happening *to* us that determines our feelings, but what is happening *in* us. As we discuss attitude this week, bear in mind what you have written, and try to determine whether your attitude is helping you be a better leader or hindering you from becoming all you can be.

Day 1

Your Attitude:
Your Most Important Asset

Our attitudes may not be the assets that make us great leaders, but without good ones we will never reach our full potential. Our attitudes are the "and then some" that allows us the little extra edge over those whose thinking is wrong.

Does your leadership reflect good technical skills, a good attitude, or both? How can you play off the stronger asset?

Example: Use my positive attitude about my job to learn more skills that can help me in my job.

Robert Half International, a San Francisco consulting firm, asked vice presidents and personnel directors at one hundred of America's largest companies to name the single greatest reason for firing an employee. The responses are very interesting and underscore the importance of attitude in the business world:

- **Incompetence:** 30 percent.

- **Inability to get along with other workers:** 17 percent.

- **Dishonesty or lying:** 12 percent.

- **Negative attitude:** 10 percent.

- **Lack of motivation:** 7 percent.

- **Failure or refusal to follow instructions:** 7 percent.

- **All other reasons:** 8 percent.

Notice that although incompetence ranked first on the list, the next five were all attitude problems. The Carnegie Institute analyzed the records of ten thousand persons and concluded that 15 percent of success is due to technical training. The other 85 percent is due to personality, and the primary personality trait identified by the research is attitude.

Our attitudes determine what we see and how we handle our feelings.

These two factors greatly determine our success. Read the following examples and notice how you see situations and how you handle your feelings.

WHAT YOU SEE

Psychology 101 taught me that we see what we are prepared to see. Nell Mohney, in her book *Beliefs Can Influence Attitudes*, pointedly illustrates this truth. Mohney tells of a double-blind experiment conducted in the San Francisco Bay area. The principal of a school called three professors together and said, "Because you three teachers are the finest in the system and you have the greatest expertise, we're going to give you ninety high-IQ students. We're going to let you move these students through this next year at their own pace and see how much they can learn." Everyone was delighted—faculty and students alike.

Over the next year, the professors and the students thoroughly enjoyed themselves. The professors were teaching the brightest students; the students were benefiting from the close attention and instruction of highly skilled teachers. By the end of the experiment, the students had achieved from 20 to 30 percent more than the other students in the whole area.

The principal called the teachers in and told them, "I have a confession to make. I have to confess that you did not have ninety of the most intellectually prominent students. They were run-of-the-mill students. We took ninety students at random from the system and gave them to you."

The teachers said, "This means that we are exceptional teachers." The principal continued, "I have another confession. You're not the brightest of the teachers. Your names were the first three names drawn out of a hat."

The teachers asked, "What made the difference? Why did ninety students perform at such an exceptional level for a whole year?"[2]

The difference, of course, was the teachers' expectations. Our expectations have a great deal to do with our attitudes. And these expectations may be totally false, but they will determine our attitudes.

Are your expectations of your workers mostly positive or mostly negative? Briefly describe what you expect your workers to be able to accomplish.

HOW YOU HANDLE YOUR FEELINGS

Notice I did not say your attitudes determine how you feel. There is a great difference between how you feel and how you handle your feelings. Everyone has times when he feels bad. Our attitudes cannot stop our feelings, but they can keep our feelings from stopping us. Unfortunately, too many allow their feelings to control them.

How often do you let your emotions get the best of you? Which emotions are the most difficult for you to handle appropriately? (Examples: anger, sadness, pride)

APPLYING WHAT I'VE LEARNED

We've learned that attitude can be defined as 1) what we see and 2) how we handle our feelings.

Do you tend to see situations through positive or negative eyes?

How could changing your perspective on a current situation change how you handle that situation?

Referring to the emotions that give you the most difficulty, list some specific ways that you can begin to limit the ways that they limit you.

Day 2

The Bad Attitude

IT IS IMPROBABLE THAT A PERSON WITH A BAD ATTITUDE CAN CONTINUOUSLY BE A SUCCESS

Norman Vincent Peale relates this story in his book *Power of the Plus Factor*: Once walking through the twisted little streets of Kowloon in Hong Kong, I came upon a tattoo studio. In the window were displayed samples of the tattoos available. On the chest or arms you could have tattooed an anchor or flag or mermaid or whatever. But what struck me with force were three words that could be tattooed on one's flesh, *Born to lose*.

I entered the shop in astonishment and, pointing to those words, asked the Chinese tattoo artist, "Does anyone really have that terrible phrase, *Born to lose*, tattooed on his body?"

He replied, "Yes, sometimes."

"But," I said, "I just can't believe that anyone in his right mind would do that."

The Chinese man simply tapped his forehead and in broken English said, "Before tattoo on body, tattoo on mind."[3]

Once our minds are "tattooed" with negative thinking, our chances for long-term success diminish. We cannot continue to function in a manner that we do not truly believe about ourselves. Often I see people sabotage themselves because of wrong thinking.

Is your success being sabotaged by a bad attitude? Fill in the following blank with the word that best describes how you feel about your chances at success:

I believe my chances for success are _____.

It's the attitude that makes the difference. People with negative thinking may start well, have a few good days, and even have small successes. But sooner or later (it's usually sooner), their attitudes will pull them down.

WE ARE RESPONSIBLE FOR OUR ATTITUDES

Our destinies in life will never be determined by our complaining spirits or high expectations. Life is full of surprises and the adjustment of our attitudes is a life-long project.

The pessimist complains about the wind.
The optimist expects it to change.
The leader adjusts the sails.

We choose what attitudes we have right now. And it's a continuing choice. I am amazed at the large number of adults who fail to take responsibility for their attitudes. When they're grumpy and someone asks why, they'll say, "I got up on the wrong side of the bed." When failure begins to plague their lives, they'll say, "I was born on the wrong side of the tracks." When life begins to flatten out and others in the family are still climbing, they'll say, "Well, I was in the wrong birth order in my family." When their marriages fail, they believe they married the wrong person. When someone else gets a promotion they wanted, it's because they were in the wrong place at the wrong time. Do you notice something? They are blaming everyone else for their problems.

If you tend to blame your problems on someone or something else, how can you change your attitude? What do you see as the reccurring theme in your gripes? What can you do to take control?

The greatest day in life is when we take total responsibility for our attitudes. That's the day we truly grow up.

APPLYING WHAT I'VE LEARNED

All too often, we let our bad attitudes control the way we treat others. To be a more effective leader, you must learn to adopt a good attitude and to take responsibility for your success or failure. Read the following poem and write a brief statement reflecting on how you will choose to maintain a good attitude in any situation:

> We cannot choose how many years we will live, but we can
> choose how much life those years will have.
> We cannot control the beauty of our face, but we can
> control the expression on it.
> We cannot control life's difficult moments, but we can
> choose to make life less difficult.
> We cannot control the negative atmosphere of the world,
> but we can control the atmosphere of our minds.
> Too often, we try to choose and control things we cannot.
> Too seldom, we choose to control what we can . . . our attitude.[4]

Day 3

A Leader's Attitude

IT'S NOT WHAT HAPPENS TO ME THAT MATTERS BUT WHAT HAPPENS IN ME

What is happiness?

Happiness is

Hugh Downs says that a happy person is not a person with a certain set of circumstances, but rather a person with a certain set of attitudes. Too many people believe that happiness is a condition. When things are going great, they're happy. When things are going bad, they're sad. Some people have what I call "destination disease." They think that happiness can be found in a position or a place. Others have what I call "someone sickness." They think happiness results from knowing or being with a particular person.

I am impressed with the philosophy of the following statement: "God chooses what we go through. We choose how we go through it." It describes Viktor Frankl's attitude as he was terribly mistreated in a Nazi concentration camp. His words to his persecutors have been an inspiration to millions of people. He said, "The one thing you cannot take away from me is the way I choose to respond to what you do to me. The last of one's freedoms is to choose one's attitude in any given circumstance."[5]

Many times people who have suffered adverse situations in their lives become bitter and angry. Over time, their lives will be negative and hardened toward others. The tendency for them is to point back to a difficult time and say, "That incident ruined my life." What they do not realize is that the incident called for an attitude decision—a response. Their wrong attitude choice, not the condition, ruined their lives.

Do any of your past experiences continue to haunt you with bitterness or anger? If so, what can you do to let go of that negative attitude and move forward?

C. S. Lewis said, "Every time you make a choice you are turning the control part of you, the part that chooses, into something a little different from what it was before. And taking your life as a whole, with all your innumerable choices, you are slowly turning this control thing either into a heavenly creature or into a hellish one."[6]

What does your "control thing" resemble? If it resembles a hellish one, how are you making changes? How can you start to make positive choices?

THE LEADER'S ATTITUDE HELPS DETERMINE THE ATTITUDES OF THE FOLLOWERS

Leadership is influence. People catch our attitudes just like they catch our colds—by getting close to us. As a leader, I need to possess a great attitude, not only for my own success, but also for the benefit of others. My responsibilities as a leader must always be viewed in light of the many, not just myself.

Dr. Frank Crane reminds us that a ball rebounds from the wall with precisely the force with which it was thrown against the wall. There is a law in physics to the effect that action is equal to reaction. That law is also true in the realm of influence. In fact, its effects multiply with a leader's influence. The action of a leader multiplies in reaction because there are several followers. To a smile given, many smiles return. Anger unleashed toward others results in much anger returned from many. There are few actual victims of fate. The generous are helped and the stingy are shunned.

I believe that a leader's attitude is caught by his followers more quickly than his actions. An attitude is reflected by others even when they don't follow the action. An attitude can be expressed without a word being spoken.

Do any of your followers have negative attitudes? Can any aspect of that be traced back to your attitude?

The effect of a leader's attitude on others is the main reason for the importance of considering a candidate's attitude when hiring an executive. Practicing psychologists list five areas needing significant appraisal when employees are being considered for executive promotion:

1. Ambition

2. Attitudes toward policy

3. Attitudes toward colleagues

4. Supervisory skills

5. Attitudes toward excessive demands on time and energy

A candidate who is out of balance in one or more of these areas would be likely to project a negative attitude and, therefore, prove to be a poor leader.

APPLYING WHAT I'VE LEARNED

We always have a choice, and as leaders our choices will affect our followers. What is your choice? My father, who has a wonderfully positive attitude, still reads motivational books. As he says, "My attitude does not run on automatic." List the negative attitudes within you that have influenced or are currently influencing others:

Day 4

How to Change Your Attitude

Many people seem to suffer from what Ashley Montagu, the great Rutgers anthropologist, called *psychosclerosis*. Like arteriosclerosis, which is hardening of the arteries, psychosclerosis is *hardening of the attitudes*.

David Neiswanger of the Menninger Foundation says that if each of us can be helped by science to live a hundred years, "what will it profit us if our hates and fears, our loneliness and our remorse, will not permit us to enjoy them?"

The following sections will help you to help yourself in changing your attitude.

REVIEW

Many years ago my wife, Margaret, and I bought our first house. Our limited finances forced us to find some ways of getting what we wanted without spending a great deal of money. We agreed we would work on the front yard ourselves to save labor expenses and still create a proper setting for our home. It looked great.

One day, while I was standing in our backyard, I began to realize that we had spent no time or money making the back look good. Why? Because it couldn't be seen by others as they passed our house. We were careless about the area that was hidden.

That is exactly what people do in their personal lives. Their appearances, which can be seen outwardly, are spared no expense or energy. Yet their attitudes are neglected and underdeveloped.

The following six steps will help you develop a right attitude and make a permanent change in your disposition.

THE SIX STAGES OF ATTITUDE CHANGE

1. Identify problem feelings. This is the earliest stage of awareness and the easiest to declare.

   My problem feelings are

2. Identify *problem* behavior. Now we go beneath the surface. What actions trigger negative emotions?

3. Identify problem thinking. William James said, "That which holds our attention determines our action."

   My thoughts that provoke problems are

4. *Identify right thinking.* Write down the thinking that is right and what you desire. Because your feelings come from your thoughts, you can control your feelings by changing one thing—your thoughts!

The right thoughts that I'd like to develop are

5. *Make a public commitment to right thinking.* Public commitment becomes powerful commitment.

6. *Develop a plan for right thinking.* This plan should include:
- A written definition of desired right thinking
- A way to measure progress
- A daily measuring of progress
- A person to whom you are accountable
- A daily diet of self-help materials
- Associating with right thinking people

APPLYING WHAT I'VE LEARNED

Our attitudes are not only what others can easily see but that which defines our actions. You have started your plan for right thinking. Continue developing this plan.

Write a definition of desired right thinking. (Use your statements from number 4.)

How can you measure your progress daily? Who is your accountability partner?

What resources will you read or listen to?

In addition to your accountability partner, who else should you be associating with?

Whose company should you avoid?

Day 5

A New Attitude

Once you have initialized the plan for self-improvement, you can begin to follow these steps to increase your probability of success.

RESOLVE

Whenever a leader needs to ask others to make a commitment of time, two questions must always be answered: "Can they?" (this deals with ability) and "Will they?" (this deals with attitude). The more important question of the two is "Will they?" Two other questions usually answer the "Will they?" issue. The first is, "Is the timing right?" In other words, are the conditions right to enable positive change? The second question is, "Is their temperature hot?" Are right conditions accompanied with a red-hot desire to pay the price necessary for needed change? When both questions can be answered with a resounding "Yes!" then the resolve is strong and success is possible.

Think about the people you will need to work with on an upcoming project. List them. Next, ask the two questions that will determine their ability to participate.

Names	*Can they?*	*Will they?*
	Yes No	Yes No
	Yes No	Yes No
	Yes No	Yes No

REFRAME

Denis Waitley says that the winners in life think constantly in terms of I can, I will, and I am. Losers, on the other hand, concentrate their waking thoughts on what they should have done or what they didn't do. If we don't like our performances, then we must first change the picture.

Reframing your attitude means:

> I may not be able to change the world I see around me,
> but I can change the way I see the world within me.

REENTER

As you begin changing your thinking, start immediately to change your behavior. Begin to act the part of the person you would like to become. Take action on the behavior you admire by making it your behavior. Too many people want to feel, then take action. This never works.

You can't wait on motivation. "Motivation," says John Bruner, "is like love and happiness. It's a by-product. When you're actively engaged in doing something, the motivation to keep on doing it sneaks up and zaps you when you least expect it." As Harvard psychologist Bruner says, you're more likely to act yourself into feeling than feel yourself into action. So act! Whatever it is you know you should do, do it.

List the specific actions you want to take in order to improve your attitude. For example, if you are angry, practice kindness. If you are greedy, practice generosity.

REPEAT

Paul Meier said, "Attitudes are nothing more than habits of thought, and habits can be acquired. An action repeated becomes an attitude realized." Once, while leading a conference, I was asked for a simple plan to help a person change some wrong attitudes. I recommended two things to help her change her attitude:

1. Say the right words,
    Read the right books,
    Listen to the right tapes,
    Be with the right people,
    Do the right things,
    Pray the right prayer.

2. Do number one every day, not just once or only when you feel like it, and watch your life change for the better.

RENEWAL

Fortunately, over a period of time, a positive attitude can replace a negative one. Again, let me emphasize that the battle is never over, but it is well worth our efforts. The more that negative thoughts are weeded out and replaced by positive ones, the more personal renewal we will experience.

APPLYING WHAT I'VE LEARNED

Make a resolution today to put into action the steps you have learned for adjusting your attitude. List four encouraging statements that you will commit to using when faced with a challenge. The phrase can be as simple as: *I know we can do this!*

1. _____

2. _____

3. _____

4. _____

ATTITUDE
DISCUSSION QUESTIONS

1. Do you agree that a bad attitude is incompatible with success? Why?

2. What is your reaction to the statistic indicating that 70 percent of people who lose their jobs get fired due to their attitudes?

3. Think about the people you've worked with in the past. What were the characteristics of the people who were enjoying long-term success? Describe them.

4. What were the characteristics of those who didn't seem to make any progress? What percentage of those characteristics had to do with attitude?

5. In this week's lesson, one story made the point that before a tattoo goes on the skin, one exists on the mind. Another way to say that is that who you are is what you see. What things have been "tattooed" on your mind that make you who you are?

6. When it comes to your attitude, which of the following is most likely to trip you up? Why?
   A) Problem feelings
   B) Problem behavior
   C) Problem thinking

7. Why is getting along with others especially important for leaders?

8. How can leaders effectively balance modeling a positive attitude with the need to give constructive criticism or handle discipline with their people?

9. Leaders don't complain about the wind—they adjust the sails. What are some of the ways leaders can do that for themselves and for their people?

Week 7

Developing Your Most Appreciable Asset: *People*

INTRODUCTION

The one who influences others to follow only is a leader with certain limitations. The one who influences others to lead others is a leader without limitations. As Andrew Carnegie said, no man will make a great leader who wants to do it all himself or to get all the credit for doing it.

Guy Ferguson puts it this way:

> To know how to do a job is the accomplishment of labor;
> To be available to tell others is the accomplishment of the teacher;
> To inspire others to do better work is the accomplishment of management;
> To be able to do all three is the accomplishment of true leaders.

I have observed that there are three levels of people/work skills:

- **Level 1:** The person who works better with people is a follower.

- **Level 2:** The person who helps people work better is a manager.

- **Level 3:** The person who develops better people to work is a leader.

This week will focus on the importance of developing people to share in and assist you with the implementation of your dreams as a leader. The thesis is: *The more people you develop, the greater the extent of your dreams.*

Answer the following question: Can a leader accomplish all of his goals without the help of others? Why or why not?

If a leader believes that he could accomplish all of his goals alone, then the goals probably aren't that big. One is too small a number to achieve great significance.

PRINCIPLES FOR PEOPLE DEVELOPMENT

My success in developing others will depend on how well I deal with each of the following:

- **Value of people.** This is an issue of my attitude.

- **Commitment to people.** This is an issue of my time.

- **Integrity with people.** This is an issue of my character.

- **Standard for people.** This is an issue of my vision.

- **Influence over people.** This is an issue of my leadership.

For several years I have developed people under my leadership, and I have taught and observed other leaders who excelled in this vital area. I have discovered that there are three areas in which successful people-developers are different from those who are not successful in developing others. Successful people-developers . . .

1. Make the right assumptions about people.

2. Ask the right questions about people.

3. Give the right assistance to people.

This week we will be talking about these areas in detail. Specifically we will discuss:

- A leader's assumptions

- Motivate or intimidate

- Asking the right questions

- Assistance

- People development principles

People who are placed in leadership positions, but attempt to do it all alone, will someday come to the same conclusion as the brick layer who tried to move about five hundred pounds of bricks from the top of a four-story building to the sidewalk below. His problem was that he tried to do it alone.

In his own words, as taken from the insurance claim form, he explains what happened: "It would have taken too long to carry the bricks down by hand, so I decided to put them in a barrel and lower them by a pulley which I had fastened to the top of the building. After tying the rope securely at the ground level, I then went up to the top of the building. I fastened the rope around the barrel, loaded it with the bricks, and swung it out over the sidewalk for the descent.

"Then I went down to the sidewalk and untied the rope, holding it securely to guide the barrel down slowly. But, since I weigh only one hundred and forty pounds, the five-hundred-pound load jerked me from the ground so fast that I didn't have time to think of letting go of the rope. And as I passed between the second and third floors, I met the barrel coming down. This accounts for the bruises and lacerations on my upper body.

"I held tightly to the rope until I reached the top, where my hand became jammed in the pulley. This accounts for my broken thumb. At the same time, however, the barrel hit the sidewalk with a bang and the bottom fell out. With the weight of the bricks gone, the barrel weighed only about forty pounds. Thus, my one-hundred-forty-pound body began a swift descent, and I met the empty barrel coming up. This accounts for my broken ankle.

"Slowed only slightly, I continued the descent and landed on the pile of bricks. This accounts for my sprained back and broken collarbone. At this point, I lost my presence of mind completely and let go of the rope. And the empty barrel came crashing down on me. This accounts for my head injuries.

"As for the last question on the form, 'What would you do if the same situation arose again?' please be advised that I am finished trying to do the job alone."

A leader understands that doing it alone is often a bad decision.

Day 1

A Leader's Assumptions

Motivating others has always been one of my personal strengths. For years I was asked, "John, how do you motivate people?" My pat answers were things like, "Stay enthusiastic"; "encourage others"; "lead the way"; "believe in people." I would watch others follow my advice and be successful for a short time, only to fall back into the old habit patterns and the resulting low morale.

Observing this downward cycle, I would ask myself why the people who took my advice couldn't continually motivate others. Then one day it hit me! I was giving them the *fruit* of my motivational gifts, but not the *root*.

The root of my motivation is in my assumptions about others. My assumptions about others are what allow me to continually motivate and develop them. In fact, a leader having the right assumptions about people is the key factor in their continual development.

What kind of assumptions do you have about your workers? In the spaces provided, list some of the things you feel your followers are able or unable to do. What do you assume they need or want? What are their motivations?

My followers are able to _____

My followers are unable to _____

They need _____

They want _____

They are motivated by _____

An assumption is an opinion that something is true. My assumptions about people largely determine how I treat them. Why? What I assume about people is what I look for. What I look for is what I find. What I find influences my response. Therefore, negative assumptions about others will stimulate negative leadership of them. Positive assumptions about others will stimulate positive leadership of them.

Here are several assumptions about people that I have found to be extremely valuable.

EVERYONE WANTS TO FEEL WORTHWHILE

The most successful teachers, writers, managers, politicians, philosophers, and leaders instinctively know this simple fact: Every person in the world is hungry. Yes, every person in this world is hungry for something, be it recognition, companionship, understanding, love—the list is endless. One thing I always find on a list of people's needs is the desire to feel worthwhile. People want to feel important!

How are you feeding your team's need for significance?

Donald Laird says to always help people increase their own self-esteem. Develop your skills in making other people feel important. There is hardly a higher compliment you can pay an individual than to help that person be useful and find satisfaction and significance. I believe that!

EVERYONE NEEDS AND RESPONDS
TO ENCOURAGEMENT

In my many years developing people, I have yet to find a person who did not do better work and put forth greater effort under a spirit of approval than under a spirit of criticism. Encouragement is oxygen to the soul.

Do you have a spirit of criticism or a spirit of approval? Monitor how often you criticize compared to how often you compliment.

PEOPLE "BUY INTO" THE LEADER BEFORE THEY "BUY INTO" HIS OR HER LEADERSHIP

Too often we expect people to be loyal to the *position* of a leader instead of to the *person* who occupies that position. Organizational charts do not motivate people. People respond to other people. The first thing a leader must declare is not authority because of rights, but authority because of relationships. People do not care how much you know until they know how much you care. You've got to give loyalty down before you receive loyalty up. If people do not believe in their leader, anything will hinder them from following. If people believe in their leader, nothing will stop them.

How can you show your followers that you care about them?

MOST PEOPLE DO NOT KNOW HOW TO BE SUCCESSFUL

Most people think success is luck, and they keep trying to win the lottery of life. But success is really the result of planning. Most people think success is instantaneous. They look at it as a moment, an event, or a place in time. It's not. Success is really a process. Most people think that success is learning how to never fail. But that's not true. Success is learning from failure.

Do you model a right understanding of success? How can you use this knowledge to help others become successful?

MOST PEOPLE ARE NATURALLY MOTIVATED

Just watch a one year old try to explore and find out what is in a house. That is natural motivation. My observation is that most adults begin an endeavor with a desire to participate, but are often de-motivated and then must be re-motivated to participate.

What influences de-motivate you? How can you eliminate these influences? (Tomorrow's lesson will go into this more.)

APPLYING WHAT I'VE LEARNED

People have a way of living up or down to your opinion of them. By assuming the best of people, we can gain better results from people. Take one person from your team and apply these "assumptions" to them.

Name: _____

_____makes this person feel important.

I show genuine concern for this person by _____

I am helping this person in a process of success by _____

_____

I create a motivational environment by _____

_____

Day 2

Motivate or Intimidate

The true secret of motivation is creating an environment in which people are free from the influences that de-motivate. Today, we will look at what motivates and what de-motivates your workers.

WHAT MOTIVATES PEOPLE

Significant contributions. People want to join in a group or pursue a cause that will have lasting impact. They need to see that what they are doing is not wasted effort, but is making a contribution. People must see value in what they are doing. Motivation comes not by activity alone, but by the desire to reach the end result.

Does each member of your team know the impact of their contribution? How?

Goal participation. People support what they create. Being part of the goal-setting process is motivating and it allows people to feel needed. They like to feel they are making a difference. When people have given input, they have a stake in the issue. They own it and support it. Seeing goals become reality and helping to shape the future are fulfilling. Goal participation builds team spirit, enhances morale, and helps everyone feel important.

Do your team members participate in setting goals, or are goals handed down to them?

Positive dissatisfaction. Someone said that *dissatisfaction* is the one-word definition for *motivation*. Dissatisfied people are highly motivated people, for they see the need for immediate change. They know something is wrong and often know what needs to be done. Dissatisfaction can inspire change or it can lead to a critical spirit. It can lead to apathy or stir one to action. The key is harnessing this energy toward effective change.

What outlet do your people have for communicating a need for change to you? Are they allowed to come up with new ways to do things?

Recognition. People want to be noticed. They want credit for personal achievements and appreciation for their contributions. Often giving recognition is another way of saying thanks. Personal accomplishment is motivating, but it is much more so when someone notices the accomplishment and gives worth to it. Recognition is one way to give meaning to a person's existence.

How does your organization recognize personal achievement?

Clear expectations. People are motivated when they know exactly what they are to do and have the confidence that they can do it successfully. No one wants to jump into a task that is vague or a job whose description is uncertain. Motivation rises in a job when the goals, expectations, and responsibilities are clearly understood. When delegating responsibility, be sure to give the necessary authority to carry out the task. People perform better when they have some control over their work and their time.

When you delegate, do your people know what they're supposed to do and how they're expected to do it?

WHAT DE-MOTIVATES PEOPLE

Certain behavior patterns can be de-motivating. We sometimes behave in these ways without realizing the negative influences they have on others. Here's how to avoid de-motivating behavior.

How to avoid de-motivating others:
Don't belittle anyone. Public criticism and cutting conversations, even in jest, can hurt. We must be alert and sensitive. Taken to the extreme, belittling can destroy a person's self-esteem and self-confidence. If you have to give criticism, remember that it takes nine positive comments to balance one negative correction.

Don't manipulate anyone. No one likes to feel maneuvered or used. Manipulation, no matter how slight, tears down the walls of trust in a relationship. We gain more by being honest and transparent than we do by being cunning and crafty. Build people up through affirmation and praise, and they'll be motivated and loyal. Remember, give and it shall be given to you.

Don't be insensitive. Make people your priority. People are our greatest resources; therefore, take time to know and care about them. This means being responsive in conversation, never appearing preoccupied with self or in a hurry. Stop talking and develop the art of really listening. Quit thinking of what you will say next, and begin to hear not only what they say, but also how they feel. Your interest in even insignificant matters will demonstrate your sensitivity.

Don't discourage personal growth. Growth is motivating, so encourage your staff to stretch. Give them opportunities to try new things and acquire new skills. We should not feel threatened by the achievements of others, but should be very supportive of their successes. Allow your staff to succeed and fail. Build the team-spirit approach that says, "If you grow, we all benefit."

Are there resources or habits you have formed in your own personal growth plan that would be beneficial to share with your team?

APPLYING WHAT I'VE LEARNED

Check yourself. When you read through the de-motivating descriptions, did you recognize any past behavior? If so, what steps can you take to change this behavior? You may want to ask your accountability partner from last week for feedback.

Day 3

Asking the Right Questions

Sometimes, before we can make accurate and positive assumptions about people, we need to ask the right questions about ourselves. Here are six to start with:

AM I BUILDING PEOPLE OR AM I BUILDING MY DREAM AND USING PEOPLE TO DO IT?

Answering this question will help you discover your motives as a leader. There is a slight but significant difference between manipulation and motivation:

> Manipulation is moving together for *my* advantage.
> Motivation is moving together for *mutual* advantage.

DO I CARE ENOUGH TO CONFRONT PEOPLE WHEN IT WILL MAKE A DIFFERENCE?

Confrontation is very difficult for most people. If you feel uneasy just reading the word *confront*, I'd like to suggest that you substitute the word *clarify*. Clarify the issue instead of confronting the person. Once you have decided to "clarify" an issue with someone, follow these ten commandments.

The Ten Commandments of Confrontation

1. Do it privately, not publicly.

2. Do it as soon as possible. That is more natural than waiting a long time.

3. Speak to one issue at a time. Don't overload the person with a long list of issues.

4. Once you've made a point, don't keep repeating it.

5. Deal only with actions the person can change. If you ask the person to do something he or she is unable to do, frustration builds in your relationship.

6. Avoid sarcasm. Sarcasm signals that you are angry at people, not at their actions, and may cause them to resent you.

7. Avoid words like *always* and *never*. They usually detract from accuracy and make people defensive.

8. Present criticisms as suggestions or questions if possible.

9. Don't apologize for the confrontational meeting. Doing so detracts from it and may indicate you are not sure you had the right to say what you did.

10. Don't forget the compliments. Use what I call the "sandwich" in these types of meetings: Compliment—Confront—Compliment.

AM I LISTENING TO PEOPLE WITH MORE THAN MY EARS; AM I HEARING MORE THAN WORDS?

This is a test. Give yourself four points if the answer to the following questions is Always; three points for Usually; two for Rarely; and one for Never.

_____   Do I allow the speaker to finish without interrupting?

_____   Do I listen "between the lines"; that is, for the subtext?

_____   When writing a message, do I listen for and write down the key facts and phrases?

_____ Do I repeat what the person just said to clarify the meaning?

_____ Do I avoid getting hostile and/or agitated when I disagree with the speaker?

_____ Do I tune out distractions when listening?

_____ Do I make an effort to seem interested in what the other person is saying?

Scoring

26 or higher: You are an excellent listener.
22–25: Better than average score.
18–21: Room for improvement here.
17 or lower: Get out there right away and practice your listening.[1]

DO I KNOW THE MAJOR STRENGTHS
OF THIS INDIVIDUAL?

Anyone who continually has to work in areas of personal weakness instead of personal strength will not stay motivated. If individuals have been grinding away at tasks assigned in their weak areas and you reassign them to work in areas of strength, you'll see a dramatic increase in natural motivation.

HAVE I PLACED A HIGH PRIORITY ON THE JOB?

People tend to stay motivated when they see the importance of the things they are asked to do. The five most encouraging words in an organization are: "It will make a difference." The five most discouraging words in an organization are: "It won't make any difference."

HAVE I SHOWN THE VALUE THE PERSON
WILL RECEIVE FROM THIS RELATIONSHIP?

People tend to stay motivated when they see the value to them of the things they are asked to do. The simple fact is when we hear an announcement, see a commercial, or are asked to make a commitment, a small voice in the back of our minds asks, "What's in it for me?"

APPLYING WHAT I'VE LEARNED

Go back and ask yourself the previous six questions. Answer honestly, taking time to reflect if necessary.

Day 4
Assistance

Successful people-developers give the right assistance to their subordinates. Today, we will look at four specific ways of assisting people.

I NEED TO WORK OUT THEIR STRENGTHS AND WORK ON THEIR WEAKNESSES

Some of the most capable people in an organization never utilize their greatest strengths. They may be locked into what management considers important jobs, and they may do them well. But they may never get an opportunity to do what they can do best. When this happens, everybody loses. The person loses because of lack of opportunity and lack of job satisfaction; the organization loses because it wastes some of its most valuable assets. The whole venture operates at less than capacity.

Can you think of any worker under your supervision who seems to be less fruitful than he could be?_____

If so, what other type of operation could this person perform that may be more beneficial to the organization?

I MUST GIVE THEM MYSELF

You can *impress* people at a distance but you can *impact* them only up close.

1. List all the people you spent thirty minutes with this week.

2. Did you initiate the time, or did they?

3. Did you have an agenda before the meeting?

4. Was the meeting for the purpose of relationships, communication, or development?

5. Was it a win-win meeting?

6. Was it with the influential top 20 percent or the lower 80 percent?

Love everyone, but give yourself to the top 20 percent in your organization. Encourage the many; mentor the few. Be transparent with them. Develop a plan for their growth. Become a team.

I MUST GIVE THEM OWNERSHIP

As we saw in Week 5, people participate more and take more responsibility when they have ownership of a task or project.

As Sidney J. Harris believes:

> People want to be appreciated, not impressed.
>   They want to be regarded as human beings,
> Not as sounding boards for other people's egos.
>   They want to be treated as an end in themselves,
> Not as a means toward the gratification of another's vanity.

I MUST GIVE THEM EVERY CHANCE FOR SUCCESS

My responsibility as a leader is to provide assistance for those who work with me by giving them:

- An excellent atmosphere to work in. It should be positive, warm, open, creative, and encouraging.

- The right tools to work with. Do not hire excellent people to do excellent work with average tools.

- A continual training program to work under. Growing employees make growing companies.

- Excellent people to work for. Develop a team. Coming together is the beginning. Working together is success.

- A compelling vision to work toward. Allow your people to work for something larger than themselves.

Great leaders always give their people a head start over those who work under an average leader. Excellent leaders add value to their people and help them become better than they would be if they worked alone. The first question a leader should ask is: "How can I help make those around me more successful?" When that answer is found and implemented, everyone wins!

APPLYING WHAT I'VE LEARNED

How do you assist those who are under your supervision? Of the four suggestions discussed, which area is your weakest?_____

In the space provided, record specific steps that you can take to improve in that area of assistance.

Day 5

People Development Principles

As we conclude this week, I want to give you several final principles of people development.

PEOPLE DEVELOPMENT TAKES TIME

Andrew Carnegie was once the wealthiest man in America. At one time, he had forty-three millionaires working for him. A reporter asked Carnegie how he hired forty-three millionaires. Carnegie responded that those men were not millionaires when they started working for him, but had become millionaires as a result. The reporter then asked how Carnegie had developed these men to become so valuable to him that he would pay them so much money. Carnegie replied that men are developed the same way gold is mined. When gold is mined, several tons of dirt must be moved to get an ounce of gold, but one doesn't go into the mine looking for dirt. One goes in looking for gold.

Are you looking for gold in your followers? Once you find their raw talents, how do you refine them?

PEOPLE SKILLS ARE ESSENTIAL FOR SUCCESS

Most chief executives of major companies, when asked what one single characteristic is most needed by those in leadership positions, replied, "The ability to work with people." Teddy Roosevelt said, "The most important single ingredient to the formula of success is knowing how to get along with people." John Rockefeller, who built giant corporations, stated that he would pay more for the ability to deal with people than any other ability under the sun.

The Center for Creative Leadership in Greensboro, North Carolina, studied 105 successful executives and discovered the following:

- They admitted their mistakes and accepted the consequences, rather than trying to blame others.

- They were able to get along with a wide variety of people.

- They had strong interpersonal skills, sensitivity to others, and tact.

- They were calm and confident, rather than moody and volatile.

Unsuccessful executives tended to be too tough, abusive, sarcastic, aloof, or unpredictable. Their worst fault was being insensitive to others.

BE A MODEL THAT OTHERS CAN FOLLOW

The number one motivational principle in the world is: *People do what people see.* The speed of the leader determines the speed of the followers. Followers will never go any farther than their leader. For years I have followed and taught this process for developing others:

Action	Result
I do it:	I model.
I do it and you are with me:	I mentor.
You do it and I am with you:	I monitor.
You do it:	You move forward.
You do it and someone is with you:	We multiply.

LEAD OTHERS BY LOOKING THROUGH THEIR EYES

Henry Wadsworth Longfellow said, "We judge ourselves by what we feel capable of doing; while others judge us by what we have already done." Any leader who successfully deals with a group of people realizes that they each have their own agenda and perception of how things are.

These questions will help you discover another person's agenda in a variety of situations:

- Background question: What is this person's history with this organization or another?

- Temperament question: What is this person's primary and secondary temperament?

- Security question: Is this, in any way, affecting the individual's job?

- Relationship question: How is he or she related to me, or someone else, organizationally?

- Motive question: What is the real reason this is on his or her agenda?

- Potential question: Does this person or issue merit the leader's time and energy?

LEADERS MUST CARE FOR PEOPLE BEFORE THEY CAN DEVELOP THEM

Teleometrics International studied the perception high-achieving executives have of the people in their organizations compared to low-achieving executives. Their results were reported in the *Wall Street Journal*. Of the 16,000 executives studied, the 13 percent identified as "high achievers" tended to care about people as well as profits. Average achievers concentrated on production, while low achievers were preoccupied with their own security. High achievers viewed subordinates optimistically, while low achievers showed a basic distrust of subordinates' abilities. High achievers sought advice from their subordinates; low achievers didn't. High achievers were listeners; moderate achievers listened only to superiors; low achievers avoided communication and relied on policy manuals.

THE GREATEST POTENTIAL FOR GROWTH OF A COMPANY IS GROWTH OF ITS PEOPLE

According to William J. H. Boetcker, people divide themselves into four classes:

1. Those who always do less than they are told.

2. Those who will do what they are told, but no more.

3. Those who will do things without being told.

4. Those who will inspire others to do things.

It's up to you. As Ralph Waldo Emerson said, "Trust men and they will be true to you; treat them greatly and they will show themselves great."

APPLYING WHAT I'VE LEARNED

J. C. Staehle, after analyzing many surveys, found that the principal causes of unrest among workers are actions good leaders can avoid:

*   Failure to give credit for suggestions.

*   Failure to correct grievances.

*   Failure to encourage.

*   Criticizing employees in front of other people.

*   Failure to ask employees their opinions.

*   Failure to inform employees of their progress.

*   Favoritism.

Every issue is an example of the leader stealing or keeping ego food—the satisfaction of the need for esteem—from the worker. Check yourself and see how many times you satisfy your own esteem needs by stealing away someone else's ego food. If you find that you are taking instead of building your workers' egos, list ways you can correct this behavior.

How can you remember to give credit for suggestions?

How can you resolve grievances quickly?

How can you be an encouragement to your workers?

How can you appropriately confront your workers?

How can you involve your followers in decisions?

How can you recognize your team's progress?

How can you not show favoritism?

PEOPLE
DISCUSSION QUESTIONS

1. Everyone has one of the following natural bents when it comes to people. Which best describes you?
   A) I develop better people to work (a leader)
   B) I help people work better (a manager)
   C) I work with people (a follower)
   D) I try to stay away from people (a loner)

2. If your answer was not letter A, what must you do to improve your orientation to people?

3. This week you read that people buy into their leaders before they buy into their leadership. Do you agree with that statement? Why?

4. Based on your past experience observing leaders and working with people, what have you observed that de-motivates people?

5. According to William J. H. Boetcker, there are four kinds of people. How can you motivate each of the first two kinds of people? How can you turn the third kind into the fourth?
   A) Those who always do less than they are told
   B) Those who will do what they are told, but no more
   C) Those who will do things without being told
   D) Those who will inspire others to do things

6. People don't care how much you know until they know how much you care. What are some ways that you can show people that you care about them?

7. What does it mean to set up someone for success? What are some ways you could do that as a leader?

8. Working with people as a leader doesn't mean you spend all your time praising and motivating them. Leadership also includes confrontation. What kind of track record do you have when it comes to confronting your people?

9. How could you improve in that area of your leadership?

Week 8

The Indispensable Quality of Leadership: *Vision*

INTRODUCTION

Robert K. Greenleaf, in his book *The Servant as Leader*, says, "Foresight is the 'lead' that the leader has. Once he loses this lead and events start to force his hand, he is leader in name only. He is not leading; he is reacting to immediate events and he probably will not long be a leader. There are abundant current examples of loss of leadership which stem from a failure to foresee what reasonably could have been foreseen, and from failure to act on that knowledge while the leader has freedom to act."[1]

My observation over more than two decades has been that all effective leaders have a vision of what they must accomplish. That vision becomes the energy behind every effort and the force that pushes through all the problems. With vision:

- The leader is on a mission and a contagious spirit is felt among the crowd until others begin to rise alongside the leader.

- Unity is essential for the dream to be realized.

- Long hours of labor are given gladly to accomplish the goal.

- Individual rights are set aside because the whole is much more important than the part.

- Time flies, morale soars upward, heroic stories are told, and commitment is the watchword.

Why? Because the leader has a vision! All that is necessary to remove the excitement from the list is one word—*vision*. Without it, energy ebbs, deadlines are missed, personal agendas begin to surface, production falls, and people scatter.

The word *vision* has perhaps been overused in the last few years. The first goal of many management workshops is to develop a statement of purpose for the organization. Others will look at you oddly if you cannot recite your organization's purpose by memory and produce a card with the statement of purpose printed on it.

Why all the pressure to develop a purpose for your organization?

There are two reasons:

1. Vision becomes the distinctive, rallying cry of the organization. It is a clear statement in a competitive market that you have an important niche among all the voices clamoring for customers. It is your real reason for existence.

2. Vision becomes the new control tool, replacing the 1,000-page manual that is boxy and constrains initiative. In an age when decentralization all the way to the front line is required to survive, the vision is the key that keeps everyone focused.

WHAT YOU SEE IS WHAT YOU CAN BE

I have often asked myself: Does the vision make the leader? Or does the leader make the vision? I believe the vision comes first. I have known many leaders who lost the vision and, therefore, lost their power to lead. People do what people see. That is the greatest motivational principle in the world.

Stanford Research says that 89 percent of what we learn is visual, 10 percent of what we learn is auditory, and 1 percent of what we learn is through other senses. In other words, people depend on visual stimulation for growth. Couple a vision with a leader willing to implement that dream and a movement begins. People do not follow a dream in itself. They follow the leader who has that dream and the ability to communicate it effectively. Therefore, vision in the beginning will make a leader, but for that vision to grow and demand a following, the leader must take responsibility for it.

FOUR VISION-LEVELS OF PEOPLE

1. Some people never see it. (They are wanderers.)

2. Some people see it but never pursue it on their own. (They are followers.)

3. Some people see it and pursue it. (They are achievers.)

4. Some people see it and pursue it and help others see it. (They are leaders.)

All great leaders possess two things: They know where they are going, and they are able to persuade others to follow. This week we will be looking at:

*   Having a vision

*   Finding your vision

*   Perception of a vision

*   Probability of a vision

*   Possibility of a vision

If you already have a vision statement, write it below.

Day 1

Having a Vision

YOU SEE WHAT YOU ARE PREPARED TO SEE

This deals with perception. Konrad Adenauer was correct when he said, "We all live under the same sky, but we don't all have the same horizon."

Automobile genius Henry Ford once came up with a revolutionary plan for a new kind of engine. We know it today as the V-8. Ford was eager to get his great new idea into production. He had some men draw up the plans and presented them to the engineers.

As the engineers studied the drawings, one by one they came to the same conclusion. Their visionary boss just didn't know much about the fundamental principles of engineering. He'd have to be told gently—his dream was impossible.

Ford said, "Produce it anyway."

They replied, "But it's impossible."

"Go ahead," Ford commanded, "and stay on the job until you succeed, no matter how much time is required."

For six months they struggled with drawing after drawing, design after design. Nothing. Another six months. Nothing. At the end of the year Ford checked with his engineers, and once again they told him that what he wanted was impossible. Ford told them to keep going. They did. And they discovered how to build a V-8 engine. Henry Ford and his engineers both lived under the same sky, but they didn't all have the same horizon.

In *A Saviour for All Seasons*, William Barker relates the story of a bishop from the East Coast who many years ago paid a visit to a small, midwestern religious college. He stayed at the home of the college president, who also served as professor of physics and chemistry. After dinner the bishop declared that the millennium couldn't be far off, because just about everything about nature had been discovered and all inventions conceived.

The young college president politely disagreed and said he felt there would be many more discoveries. When the angered bishop challenged the president to name just one such invention, the president replied he was certain that within fifty years men would be able to fly.

"Nonsense!" sputtered the outraged bishop. "Only angels are intended to fly."

The bishop's name was Wright, and he had two boys at home who would prove to have greater vision than their father. Their names were Orville and Wilbur. The father and his sons lived under the same sky, but they didn't all have the same horizon.

How can this be? Why is it that two people can be in the same place at the same time and both see entirely different things? It's simple. We see what we are prepared to see, not what is. Every successful leader understands this about people and asks these questions:

1. What do others see?

2. Why do they see it that way?

3. How can I change their perception?

Think about your own followers and answer these questions:

What do they see?_____

Why do they see it that way?_____

How can I change their perception?_____

WHAT YOU SEE IS WHAT YOU GET

Bobb Biehl, in his book *Increasing Your Leadership Confidence*, says, "Keep in mind the difference between a winner's and a loser's mentality. Winners focus on winning big—not just how to win, but how to win big. Losers, however, don't focus on losing; they just focus on getting by!"[2]

Are you striving to simply survive, are you dreaming about success, or are you really out to make a truly significant difference?

If you had anything you wanted—unlimited time, unlimited money, unlimited information, unlimited staff—all the resources you could ask for, what would you do? Your answer to that question is your dream. Make it worthwhile.

Use this one-sentence mental exercise to articulate one of your dreams:

If I had_____

I would _____

APPLYING WHAT I'VE LEARNED

To be a great leader, you must have vision. What is on the horizon for you? What is your dream? If you had unlimited resources, what would you set out to accomplish? Write out your biggest dream or goal.

Day 2

Finding Your Vision

PERSONAL OWNERSHIP OF A VISION

My friend Rick Warren says, "If you want to know the temperature of your organization, put a thermometer in the leader's mouth." Leaders can never take their people farther than they have traveled. Therefore, the focus of vision must be on the leader—like leader, like people. Followers find the leader and then the vision. Leaders find the vision and then the people.

I am asked many questions when I speak at leadership conferences throughout the country. One of the most common questions asked by those in leadership positions is: "How do I get a vision for my organization?" This question is crucial. Until it is answered, a person will be a leader in name only. Although I cannot give you a vision, I can share the process of receiving one for you and those around you.

LOOK WITHIN YOU: WHAT DO YOU FEEL?

There is a vast difference between a person with a vision and a visionary person.

- A person with a vision talks little but does much.

- A visionary person does little but talks much.

175

- A person with a vision finds strength from inner convictions.

- A visionary person finds strength from outward conditions.

- A person with a vision continues when problems arise.

- A visionary person quits when the road becomes difficult.

Are you more of a visionary or a person with a vision? Why?

Great visions begin as an "inside job." It is much easier to overcome outside obstacles than the obstacle of doubt that we find within.

LOOK BEHIND YOU: WHAT HAVE YOU LEARNED?

A person without experience sees a vision idealistically. To that individual the vision alone is enough. Naively this person casts the vision to others, expecting the dream to do the work and failing to realize that a vision needs support. A person with experience learns that people buy into the leader *before* they buy into the vision. Experienced leaders realize that people are fickle and dreams are fragile. Experience has taught me these principles about vision:

- The credibility of a vision is determined by the leader.

- The acceptance of a vision is determined by the timing of its presentation.

- The value of a vision is determined by the energy and direction it gives.

- The evaluation of a vision is determined by the commitment level of people.

- The success of a vision is determined by its ownership by both the leader and the people.

What have your experiences taught you about vision casting? How are you using this wisdom to your benefit?

LOOK AROUND YOU:
WHAT IS HAPPENING TO OTHERS?

A good idea becomes great when the people are ready. The individual who is impatient with people will be defective in leadership. The evidence of strength lies not in streaking ahead, but in adapting your stride to the slower pace of others while not forfeiting your lead. If we run too far ahead, we lose our power to influence.

How do you prepare your people for the vision?

LOOK AHEAD OF YOU:
WHAT IS THE BIG PICTURE?

This question often separates leaders from managers. Leaders are concerned with the organization's basic purpose—why it exists and what it should achieve. They are not preoccupied with the "how to" or nuts and bolts aspect of the operation.

LOOK ABOVE YOU:
WHAT DOES GOD EXPECT OF YOU?

Richard E. Day said, "Every golden era in human history proceeds from the devotion and righteous passion of some single individual. There are no bona fide mass movements; it just looks that way. There is always one man who knows his God and knows where he is going."

God's gift to me is my potential. My gift back to God is what I do with that potential. I believe great leaders sense a "higher calling"—one that lifts them above themselves. What a terrible waste of life to be climbing the ladder of success only to find when you reach the top that you were leaning against the wrong building. Great visions are bigger than the person.

LOOK BESIDE YOU:
WHAT RESOURCES ARE AVAILABLE TO YOU?

A vision should be greater than the person who has it. Its accomplishment must be the result of many people bringing many resources to the job. The experienced leader is always looking for others to make the dream come true.

Too often leaders hesitate to test the commitment levels of those around them. What is the result? They are never sure where the project stands, or where their people stand. Are you hesitant in testing your people? How can you overcome this fear?

APPLYING WHAT I'VE LEARNED

Has your vision changed since the start of this week? Are you dreaming big and looking in the right places? If you now have a vision or if you have revised your previous vision, write your new vision statement below.

Day 3

Perception of a Vision

A vision is a clear picture of what the leader sees his or her group being or doing. According to a survey reported by *Leadership* magazine, communicating a vision is one of the most frustrating areas of leading an organization.

UNDERSTANDING WHAT HINDERS A VISION

We see things not as they are, but as we are. Therefore, when a vision is hindered, it is usually a people problem. There are ten types of people who usually hinder the vision of the organization.

1. Limited leaders. Everything rises and falls on leadership. That statement is certainly true with vision-casting. A limited leader will lack either the vision or the ability to successfully pass it on.

2. Concrete thinkers. George Bernard Shaw said, "Some men see things as they are and say, 'Why?' [concrete thinker]. I dream of things that never were and say 'Why not?' [creative thinker]."

3. Dogmatic talkers. Many visions aren't realized because of strong, dogmatic people. To be absolutely certain about something, one must know either everything or nothing about it. Most of the time, the dogmatist knows nothing but conventionally says something.

4. Continual losers. Many people look at their past failures and fear the risk of pursuing a vision. Their motto is, "If at first you don't succeed, destroy all the evidence that you've tried." They also destroy everyone's attempt to ever try again.

5. Satisfied sitters. People strive for comfort, predictability, and security in life. On the heels of comfort comes complacency; of predictability, boredom; and of security, no vision. A nest is good for a robin while it is an egg. But it is bad for a robin when it has wings. It's a good place to be hatched in, but it's a poor place to fly in. It's always sad when people don't want to leave the nests of their lives.

6. Tradition lovers. John F. Parker, in *Roll Call,* tells the story that for more than twenty years, for no apparent reason, an attendant stood at the foot of the stairway leading to the British House of Commons. At last someone checked and discovered that the job had been held in the attendant's family for three generations. It seems it originated when the stairs were painted and the current attendant's grandfather was assigned the task of warning people not to step on the wet paint.

7. Census takers. Some people never feel comfortable stepping out of the crowd. They desire to be a part of, not apart from, the group. These people will embrace the vision only when the majority does. They are never in front. Harry C. McKown said, "True leaders are always in the minority because they are thinking ahead of the present majority. Even when the majority catches up, these leaders will have moved ahead and so, again, will be in the minority."[3]

8. Problem perceivers. Some people can see a problem in every solution. Interestingly, some people think the ability to see problems is a mark of maturity. Not so. It's the mark of a person without a vision. These people abort great visions by presenting problems without any solutions.

9. Self-seekers. People who live for themselves are in a mighty small business. They also never accomplish much. Great goals are reached only by the united effort of many. Selfish people are vision-busters.

10. Failure forecasters. Some people have a faculty for touching the wrong keys. From the finest instrument, they extract only discord. All their songs are in a minor key. They send the note of pessimism everywhere. The shadows dominate all their pictures. Their outlook is always gloomy, times are always bad, and money is tight. Everything in them seems to be contracting; nothing in their lives expands or grows.

I love the Chinese proverb that states, "Man who says 'it cannot be done' should not interrupt man who is doing it."

APPLYING WHAT I'VE LEARNED

Understanding what type of people you are working with will greatly increase your ability to effect change. Evaluate your followers. List their names, followed by the vision hindrance(s) that they present you with.

Name   **Hindrance to Vision**

Day 4

Probability of a Vision

SETTING THE PROPER ENVIRONMENT

Perception (the small picture) is not a level to stay on. By knowing people and the keys to their lives, the leader can move up to probability (the next picture). Probability is seeing what will be with the eyes of discernment.

It is essential for the leader to influence what will be seen by the people. Remember, if only the leader and a few others see the possibilities, then only they will know if the proper environment has been set to take others into the vision area.

The following steps will set that environment correctly:

COME ALONGSIDE THEM

Let them see your heart before they see your hope. People don't care how much you see until they see how much you care. I emphasize again: People buy into the leader before they buy into that leader's vision. Cultivate trust. Be transparent and patient. Start where they are by seeing through their eyes. Seek to find their hopes and dreams. Begin building a bridge between the vision of the organization and their personal goals. Done correctly, both can be accomplished. Go for the win-win. Remember, when you help people get what they want, they will help you get what you want. This can be accomplished only by building strong relationships with people.

PAINT THE PICTURE FOR THEM

One time I read that a great teacher never strives to explain his vision; he simply invites you to stand beside him and see for yourself. I agree with the relationship part of this statement, but I believe great leaders explain their vision by painting a picture for the people.

Every great vision has certain ingredients, and the great leader makes the people understand, appreciate, and "see" them:

Horizon

A leader's vision of the horizon allows people to see the heights of their possibilities. Each individual will determine how high he or she wants to go. Your responsibility is to put plenty of sky into the picture. Paul Harvey said that a blind man's world is bounded by the limits of his touch; an ignorant man's world by the limits of his knowledge; a great man's world by the limits of his vision.

Sun

This element represents warmth and hope. Light brings out the optimism in people. A prime function of a leader is to keep hope alive. Napoleon said, "Leaders are dealers in hope."

Mountains

Every vision has its challenges. Edwin Land, founder of Polaroid, said, "The first thing you do is teach the person to feel that the vision is very important and nearly impossible. That draws out the drive in the winner."

Birds

This element represents freedom and the spirit of man. Watching an eagle rise causes you to feel your own spirit soar. George S. Patton said, "Wars may be fought with weapons, but it is the spirit of the men who fight and of the man who leads that gains victory."[4]

Flowers

The journey toward the realization of any great vision takes time. Make sure the scenery includes rest stops—places to smell flowers and become refreshed mentally and physically. Success is the progressive realization of a predetermined, worthwhile goal.

Path

People need direction, a place to begin, and a path to follow. A traveler through a rugged country asked his Indian guide, "How are you able to pick your way over these jagged peaks, by treacherous trails, without ever losing your direction?"

The guide answered, "I have the near look and the far vision. With the one I see what is directly ahead of me; with the other I guide my course by the stars."[5]

Yourself

Never paint the vision without placing yourself in the picture. This will show your commitment to the vision and your desire to walk with the people through the process. They need a model to follow. As Warren R. Austin said in *UN World*, "If you would lift me, you must be on higher ground."

Why should a leader paint the picture and place these essentials in it? Roger von Oech, in his book *A Kick in the Seat of the Pants*, gives an excellent answer: "Take a look around where you're sitting and find five things that have blue in them. Go ahead and do it.

1.

2.

3.

4.

5.

"With a 'blue' mind-set, you'll find that blue jumps out at you: a blue book on the table, a blue pillow on the couch, blue in the painting on the wall, and so on. In like fashion, you've probably noticed that after you buy a new car, you promptly see that make of car everywhere. That's because people find what they are looking for."[6]

The leader helps the people develop this sensitivity and an eye for knowing what to look for. If the picture is painted clearly and shown continually, soon others will begin to see how it fits into everything they do. They will have a vision mind-set.

PUT THE THINGS THEY LOVE IN THE PICTURE

Put what is important to the people within the frame of the vision and you will have transferred the vision to the people.

APPLYING WHAT I'VE LEARNED

You should be able to paint a picture of your vision to others. Use your vision statement and brainstorm ways you can complete the picture.

Horizon: What are the possibilities?

Sun: How does your vision provide hope?

Mountains: What challenges do you expect? Why is the vision worth the challenges?

Birds: How can you convey a sense of spirit when talking about your vision?

Flowers: What small celebrations do you have planned, leading up to ultimate victory?

Path: What is the starting point? How can they see the path?

Yourself: What part do you have in the vision?

Things They Love: How can you give people ownership of the vision?

Day 5

Possibility of a Vision

Today, we need to ask ourselves how to grow people to the size of the vision once they see it.

There are several steps a leader at the possibility level must take. First, the leader must seek and find winners to add to the team. These qualities of winners will guide the search:

- Winners are less sensitive to disapproval and rejection—they brush it off.

- Winners think "bottom line."

- Winners focus on the task at hand.

- Winners are not superstitious—they say, "That's life."

- Winners refuse to equate failure with self-worth.

- Winners don't restrict thinking to established, rigid patterns.

- Winners see the big picture.

- Winners welcome challenge with optimism.

- Winners don't waste time in unproductive thought.

Who are the winners on your team? How have they shown a winning attitude? How can you use these winners to influence others on your team?

Once the winners are added to the team, they join others as the major influencers in the organization. At this point, it is extremely important for the leader to spend time with the influencers to discover the "keys" to their lives. What is most valued by these influencers should be discovered. The leader's game plan to build the influencers should help them through tough personal issues; provide a time and place for them to grow; add value to their family and job; assist them in finding their strengths; and plug them into the organization.

How well do you know the "winners" on your team? How can you get to know them better?

Also, it is very important for the leader to mentor these winners. They should be exposed to great books (past and present), great places, great events, and great people. They should find great ideas in you, the leader, and they should develop a desire to pursue your interests and vision in an attempt to build a mutually beneficial relationship. When this occurs, you will find that the winners naturally pass on the vision that you hold dear for your organization and for them.

What books should your influencers be reading? Where should they be going? Who should they be meeting?

The successful leader will see on three levels:

1. *The Perceptible Level:* What is now seen—the eyes of reality. A leader listens on this level.

2. *The Probable Level:* What will be seen—the eyes of discernment. A leader leads on this level.

3. *The Possible Level:* What can be seen—the eyes of vision. A leader lives on this level.

Vision is empowering to the leader that has it. The leader with vision believes not only that what he envisions can be done, but that it must be done.

There was a study done of concentration camp survivors regarding their common characteristics. Viktor Frankl was a living answer to that question. He was a successful Viennese psychiatrist before the Nazis threw him into such a camp. Years later when giving lectures he would say: "There is only one reason I am here today. What kept me alive was you. Others gave up hope. I dreamed that some day I would be here telling you how I, Viktor Frankl, had survived Nazi concentration camps. I've never been here before, I've never given this speech before. But in my dreams I have stood before you and said these words a thousand times." It was the vision that made the difference.

As a young man I learned this poem. It is an appropriate way to end this week.

> Ah, great it is to believe the dream,
> As we stand in youth by the starry stream.
> But a greater thing is to live life through,
> And say at the end, the dream came true.

Leaders do that for themselves and for others.

APPLYING WHAT I'VE LEARNED

You began this week by writing down a vision. Look at what you wrote and reevaluate it. Is there a change that would make your vision more probable? Have you given this vision to "winners" who can aid you in implementing it? In the spaces provided, revise your original vision and begin to work on growing it in the people you lead.

VISION
DISCUSSION QUESTIONS

1. Is it possible for a person to be a leader if he or she does not possess vision?

2. What's lacking in the person who does not possess a clear vision?

3. Think about some of the truly great leaders from your lifetime or history. Pick the one you admire most. What was his or her vision? How did that vision help that person keep going when he or she faced adversity?

4. This week you read that vision can replace a thousand page manual. What is the difference between an organization that relies on rules or written procedures versus one that relies on vision?

5. For a leader, where does vision get its start—from within or outside of the leader?

6. What experiences have impacted the vision you have for yourself? Your family? Your organization? (If you lack vision, how can you discover it?)

7. How does vision involve thinking "outside the lines" or "out of the box"?

8. This week's lesson taught how to include others in a vision. Have you tried to include others in your vision in the past? If you have, how successful have you been?

9. How can you improve your ability to include others?

10. Can people expect to achieve more than they are able to envision for their lives? Why?

Week 9

The Price Tag of Leadership: *Self-Discipline*

INTRODUCTION

Let's begin this week by defining self-discipline. Complete the following sentence:

Self-discipline is

Give several examples of how you currently practice self-discipline.

Harry Truman said, "In reading the lives of great men, I found that the first victory they won was over themselves . . . Self-discipline with all of them came first."[1]

The Greek word for *self-control* comes from a root word meaning "to grip" or "take hold of." This word describes people who are willing to get a grip on their lives and take control of areas that will bring them success or failure.

Aristotle used this same word to describe "the ability to test desire by reason . . . to be resolute and ever in readiness to end natural vent and pain." He explained that people who are not controlled have strong desires that try to seduce them from the way of reason; but to succeed they must keep those desires under control.

Once, while conducting a leadership seminar, I defined discipline in the beginning of life as the choice of achieving what you really want by doing things you don't really want to do. After successfully doing this for some time, discipline becomes the choice of achieving what you really want by doing things you now want to do! I truly believe we can become disciplined and enjoy it—*after years of practicing it.*

All great leaders have understood that their number one responsibility was for their own discipline and personal growth. If they could not lead themselves, they could not lead others. Leaders can never take others farther than they have gone themselves, for no one can travel without until he or she has first traveled within. A great person will lead a great organization, but growth is only possible when the leader is willing to "pay the price" for it. Many potentially gifted leaders have stopped short of the payment line and found out that shortcuts don't pay off in the long run.

This is what Edwin Markham has to say about human worth:

> We are blind until we see
> That in the human plan
> Nothing is worth the making
> If it does not make the man.
> Why build these cities glorious
> If man unbuilded goes?
> In vain we build the world
> Unless the builder also grows.[2]

Frederick the Great of Prussia was walking on the outskirts of Berlin when he encountered a very old man walking in the opposite direction.

"Who are you?" asked Frederick.

"I am a king," replied the old man.

"A king!" laughed Frederick. "Over what kingdom do you reign?"

"Over myself," was the proud reply.

"Reigning" over yourself requires personal discipline. This week we will be looking at several topics concerning self-discipline. These topics will include:

- The process of personal discipline

- Personal organization

- Responsibility

- Accountability

- Character

As you work this week, look for ways to improve your self-discipline. A great leader will always be aware of his own limitations before he tries to correct the limitations of someone else.

Day 1

The Process of Personal Discipline

START WITH YOURSELF

A reporter once asked the great evangelist D. L. Moody which people gave him the most trouble. He answered immediately, "I've had more trouble with D. L. Moody than any man alive." The late Samuel Hoffenstein said, "Wherever I go, I go too, and spoil everything." And there is the classic Jack Paar line, "Looking back, my life seems to be one long obstacle course, with me as the chief obstacle."

My observation is that more potential leaders fail because of inner issues than outer ones. When we are foolish, we want to conquer the world. When we are wise, we want to conquer ourselves.

START EARLY

Perhaps the most valuable result of all education is the ability to make yourself do the thing you have to do, when it ought to be done, whether you like it or not. It is the first lesson that ought to be learned and, however early a man's training begins, it is probably the last lesson that he learns thoroughly.

START SMALL

What you are going to be tomorrow, you are becoming today. It is essential to begin developing self-discipline in a small way today in order to be disciplined in a big way tomorrow. Here is a plan for developing self-discipline:

A Small Plan That Will Make a Big Difference

1. List five areas in your life that lack discipline.   *Rank*   *Accountability Partner*

   _____   ____   _____

   _____   ____   _____

   _____   ____   _____

   _____   ____   _____

   _____   ____   _____

2. Rank them in order of your priority for conquering them.

3. Take them on, one at a time.

4. Secure resources, such as books and tapes, which will give you instruction and motivation to conquer each area.

5. Ask a person who models the trait you want to possess to hold you accountable for it. Write their name in the accountability partner column. (Each trait may require a different accountability partner.)

6. Spend fifteen minutes each morning getting focused in order to get control of this weak area in your life.

7. Do a five-minute checkup on yourself at midday.

8. Take five minutes in the evening to evaluate your progress.

9. Allow sixty days to work on one area before you go to the next.

10. Celebrate with the one who holds you accountable as you show continued success.

Remember, having it all doesn't mean having it all at once. It takes time. Start small and concentrate on today. The slow accumulation of disciplines will one day make a big difference.

ORGANIZE YOUR LIFE

When you are organized, you have a special power. You walk with a sure sense of purpose. Your priorities are clear in your mind. You orchestrate complex events with a masterful touch. Things fall into place when you reveal your plans. You move smoothly from one project to the next with no wasted motion. Throughout the day you gain stamina and momentum as your successes build. People believe your promises because you always follow through. When you enter a meeting, you are prepared for whatever they throw at you. When at last you show your hand, you're a winner.

How organized are you? Rate yourself on a scale of 1 to 10, with 10 representing "a place for everything and everything in its place." In what areas would you like to improve?

APPLYING WHAT I'VE LEARNED

Improving your self-discipline is a large task. As you work through your weak areas, keep your eyes on the goal. What do you hope to accomplish by adding discipline to a particular area of your life? For each weakness you listed, write out a measurable definiton of success.

	Area of weakness	**Goal**
Example:	*eating—too much and unhealthy*	*lose weight and feel better*

Day 2

Personal Organization

Today, I want to give you my top-ten list for personal organization. Applying these steps will enable you to become more organized and increase your leadership capabilities.

1. SET YOUR PRIORITIES

Two things are difficult to get people to do. The first is to do things in order of importance, and the second is to *continue* doing things in order of importance.

Major events, such as my speaking at conferences, are scheduled a year or two in advance. The last week of each month I spend two hours planning my schedule for the next thirty days. On paper I list all my major responsibilities according to importance and time needed to accomplish those tasks. As each assignment is completed in its allotted time, I check it off my monthly list.

2. PLACE PRIORITIES IN YOUR CALENDAR

Once this list is written out on paper, I give it to my personal assistant, who writes it on my calendar. This protects me from outside pressures that clamor daily for my time. This also makes me accountable to someone else who will help me stay on track.

3. ALLOW A LITTLE TIME FOR THE UNEXPECTED

The kinds of work you do will determine the amount of time you set aside for interruptions. For example, the more you interact with people, the more time you must set aside. I set aside half of a day each week on my calendar for the unexpected.

4. DO PROJECTS ONE AT A TIME

A good general fights on only one front at a time. That is also true of a good leader. A feeling of being overwhelmed is the result of too many projects clamoring for your attention. For years I have followed this simple process:

1. Itemize all that needs to be done.

2. Prioritize things in order of importance.

3. Organize each project in a folder.

4. Emphasize only one project at a time.

5. ORGANIZE YOUR WORKSPACE.

My workspace is divided into two main areas: administrative and creative. In my administrative area, I keep my calendar, company information, meeting agendas, and notes pertaining to anything other than speaking or writing. In my creative area, I have all of my books and writing files. My writing files are divided into categories: old sermons, audio club lessons, conference lessons, and research. My research files are sorted by topic, and kept within arm's reach. By having all of my materials meticulously organized, I save a tremendous amount of time.

6. WORK ACCORDING TO YOUR TEMPERAMENT

If you are a morning person, organize your most important work for the morning hours. If you are a late starter, do the opposite. However, be sure not to allow the weaknesses of your temperament to excuse you from what you know you need to do to work most effectively.

What time of the day do you work best? If you haven't already, how can you schedule your most important work during these hours? (You may need to be a little creative with this if your peak time is not during the traditional 9 to 5 workday.)

7. USE YOUR TRAVEL TIME FOR LIGHT WORK AND GROWTH

I estimate that the average person could achieve eight additional hours of personal growth and work in each week by using travel time wisely. Because I travel so often, I always have personal growth tapes in my car. If I'm not listening to tapes, then I'm using my hands-free car phone to make calls. When I am traveling a long distance, I will take along a staff member so we can discuss business and build a closer relationship.

In the following spaces, list several ways you might be able to utilize your travel time:

8. DEVELOP SYSTEMS THAT WORK FOR YOU

Bobb Biehl says, "Systems—from to-do lists and calendars to libraries and computers—are your servants. They help you do things better and quicker, and by improving them, you decrease your time expenses and increase your results." Don't fight systems. Improve them.

What system(s) could you adopt that would organize your life and save you time? (Examples: calendar, filing system, address book, personal assistant)

9. ALWAYS HAVE A PLAN FOR THOSE MINUTES BETWEEN MEETINGS

Hours can be saved by making the best use of minutes. I keep a list of things to do that can be done anywhere in very short amounts of time. There are calls to make, memos to reply to or send, reports to scan, thank-you notes to write, and communication to share. Keep handy a list of things you can do in a short time.

Write out an easy to-do list (tasks that can be done in any setting) on a separate sheet of paper or index card. Carry the list with you this week.

10. FOCUS ON RESULTS, NOT THE ACTIVITY

Remember Peter Drucker's definition of efficiency (doing things right) versus effectiveness (doing the right things)? As you spend time on personal organization, be sure to keep your focus on doing the right things.

- Work where you are the strongest 80 percent of the time.

- Work where you are learning 15 percent of the time.

- Work where you are weak 5 percent of the time.

APPLYING WHAT I'VE LEARNED

Organization skills 1–4 tie together, and *they are the basis for becoming an organized leader*. If you are not already applying all four skills, start today (if you have an assistant, include him or her in this process).

List your major responsibilities for the upcoming month. Next to each responsibility, estimate how much time it will take to complete each task (also note if there is a deadline).

Responsibility   **Time needed / Deadline**

Now, block out the correct amounts of time for each task (using your "peak" hours for the most critical work). Then either you or your assistant should fill in your calendar. Remember to "schedule" time for the unexpected.

Make a folder (either electronic or traditional) for each major project you are working on. Keep up with all correspondence and information you receive in this folder.

As you complete a task, cross it off the list and file the project folder.

Day 3

Responsibility

Today, we will look at the steps a leader must take in order to accept responsibility. Winston Churchill said, "The price of greatness is responsibility."

STEPS TOWARD RESPONSIBILITY

Be responsible for who you are. A psychologist visited a prison and asked various inmates, "Why are you here?" The answers were very revealing, even though expected. There were many of them: "I was framed"; "They ganged up on me"; "It was a case of mistaken identity"; "It was not me—it was somebody else." The psychologist wondered if one could possibly find a larger group of "innocent" people anywhere else but in prison!

Is it easy or difficult for you to accept responsibility for your actions? The last time you were corrected by someone (a supervisor, co-worker, family member, friend, police officer), what was your response?

If your initial reaction was to blame someone else or give an excuse, your defensiveness may be limiting your discipline.

Be responsible for what you can do. It is rare to find a person who will be responsible, who will follow through correctly and finish the job. But without individuals who do what they can, no matter what it takes, *nothing* would get done.

> I am only one,
> But still I am one.
> I cannot do everything,
> But still I can do something;
> And because I cannot do everything
> I will not refuse to do the
> something that I can do.[3]

Do you give your best in every situation? Ask yourself:

Am I doing my best or just enough to get by?

Is my work really a reflection of my skills and talents?

If I had a job review today, would I be up for a raise or looking for another job?

Be responsible for what you have received. John D. Rockefeller Jr. said, "I believe that every right implies a responsibility; every opportunity, an obligation; every possession, a duty." Winston Churchill said, "It is not enough that we do our best; sometimes we have to do what's required." And Jesus said, "Everyone to whom much is given, from him much will be required" (Luke 12:48).

The higher you go, the more responsible you become for your actions and the actions of your team. Have you accepted more responsibility in your current leadership role than in the role you had before? If not, how can you improve?

Be responsible to those you lead. Great leaders never set themselves above their followers except in carrying out responsibilities.

Coach Bo Schembechler tells about the third game of the 1970 season. His University of Michigan Wolverines were playing Texas A&M, and they could not move the ball. All of a sudden, Dan Dierdorf, their offensive lineman—who was probably the best in the country at that time—came rushing over to the sidelines. Fed up with the team's performance, he yelled at Schembechler in front of everyone on the sidelines. "Listen, coach! Run every play over me! Over me! Every play!" And they did. Michigan ran off-tackle six times in a row and marched right down the field. Michigan won the game.

When the game is on the line, great leaders always take responsibility for leading their teams for victory.

APPLYING WHAT I'VE LEARNED

To ensure that a task will be completed, you should keep track of the team's responsibilities and progress. If you have not already written out the requirements of each team member for the task your group is currently working on, do so below. List each person's name, their part in this task, and your responsibility to each team member (setting up a time to review progress, providing materials, giving information, etc.).

Group Task or Project Name:_____

Team member	Responsible for	Leader's responsibility
_____	_____	_____
	_____	_____
_____	_____	_____
	_____	_____
_____	_____	_____
	_____	_____
_____	_____	_____
	_____	_____

_____   _____   _____
                    _____   _____

_____   _____   _____
                    _____   _____

_____   _____   _____
                    _____   _____

_____   _____   _____
                    _____   _____

Day 4

Accountability

Plato said, "The unexamined life is not worth living." Success and power have often crowded out of the leader's life a willingness to become accountable to others. Leaders in all areas of life are increasingly falling before the public because of this problem. Why does this happen?

HUMAN NATURE CANNOT HANDLE UNCHECKED POWER

Abraham Lincoln said, "Nearly all men can stand adversity, but if you want to test a man's character, give him power." Power can be compared to a great river. While within bounds, it is both beautiful and useful. But when it overflows its banks, it destroys. The danger of power lies in the fact that those who are invested with it tend to make its preservation their first concern. Therefore, they will naturally oppose any changes in the forces that have given them this power. History tells us that power leads to the abuse of power, and abuse of power leads to the loss of power.

Name several leaders that you believe were corrupted by their power:

LEADERS CAN EASILY BE SEPARATED FROM THEIR PEOPLE

When Harry Truman was thrust into the presidency at the death of FDR, Sam Rayburn gave him some fatherly advice: "From here on out you're going to have lots of people around you. They'll try to put a wall around you and cut you off from any ideas but theirs. They'll tell you what a great man you are, Harry. But you and I both know you ain't."

List your "yes men" (those who will tell you what you want to hear) and list your "tell it like it is men" (those who will tell you what you need to hear).

Yes Men　　　　　　　　**Tell It Like It Is Men**

Hubert H. Humphrey said, "There is no party, no Chief Executive, no Cabinet, no legislature in this or any other nation, wise enough to govern without constant exposure to informed criticism." That is true for any person who occupies a leadership position.

So how does a leader remain accountable to both his position and the people he leads? The answer is that the leader develops *integrity*.

INTEGRITY

Integrity in a leader must be demonstrated daily in a number of tangible ways. These are five ways I strive to demonstrate integrity to those I lead.

1. I live what I teach. Deciding what to be is more important than deciding what to do. Often we ask young people, "What are you going to do when you grow up?" But the more important question is, "What are you going to *be*?" The character decision must be made before a career is chosen.

2. I do what I say. If I promise something to a subordinate, colleague, or superior, I want to keep my word. The Center for Creative Leadership in Greensboro, North Carolina, released a study of twenty-one high-potential executives who were terminated from their companies or forced to retire early. The one universal character flaw or unforgivable sin that always led to their downfall was a betrayal of trust. They had not done something that was promised.

3. I'm honest with others. If those who work with me ever catch me misrepresenting the facts or covering up a problem, I will instantly lose credibility. And it will not be easy to repair.

Dr. William Schultz, a noted psychologist who developed truth-in-management strategies at Procter and Gamble and NASA, says, "If people in business just told the truth, 80 to 90 percent of their problems would disappear." Trust and honesty are the means that allow individuals to cooperate, so they can all prosper.

4. I put what is best for others ahead of what is best for me. The organization I lead and those I work with must come first. When I put the organization's best interests ahead of mine, I keep integrity with those who hired me. When I put the interests of those I work with ahead of mine, I develop friendships and loyalty.

5. I'm transparent and vulnerable. Long ago I realized that in working with people, I have two choices. I can close my arms or I can open them. Both choices have strengths and weaknesses. If I close my arms, I won't get hurt, but I will not get much help either. If I open my arms I'm likely to get hurt, but I will also receive help. What has been my decision? I've opened my arms and allowed others to enjoy the journey with me. My greatest gift to others is not a job, but myself. That is true of any leader.

APPLYING WHAT I'VE LEARNED

How much time do you spend practicing integrity? Indicate your level of integrity for each of the methods discussed above.

I live what I teach _____ % of the time.

I do what I say _____% of the time.

I am honest with others _____% of the time.

I put others before myself _____% of the time.

I am vulnerable _____% of the time.

If you were low in any area, what steps can you take to make your words and deeds match up?

Day 5

Character

PAY NOW, PLAY LATER

There are two paths that people can take. They can either play now and pay later, or pay now and play later. Regardless of the choices, one thing is certain. Life will demand a payment.

My father taught me this important discipline. Each week he would lay out the chores for the next seven days. Many of them could be done any time during the week. Our goal was to complete them by Saturday noon. If we completed them, we could do something fun with the family. If someone did not complete them, fun was forfeited, and that individual stayed home to complete the chores. I needed to miss my deadline only a couple of times to realize that I needed to "pay up front" and finish my work on time.

This lesson has been valuable to me, and I taught it to my children, Elizabeth and Joel Porter. I wanted them to understand that there is no such thing as a "free lunch," that life is not a gift—it is an investment. The sooner they could take control of their desires and submit them to life's demands, the more successful they would become.

John Foster said, "A man without decision of character can never be said to belong to himself. He belongs to whatever can make captive of him." My friend Bill Klassen often reminds me that "when we pay later the price is greater!"

Do you tend to "pay now" or "pay later"? Based on your experience, make a list below of advantages and disadvantages of each strategy. In the long run, which method yields a greater return?

Pay Now:

　　　Advantages　　　　　　　　　　Disadvantages

Pay Later:

　　　Advantages　　　　　　　　　　Disadvantages

"I've never known a man worth his salt who in the long run, deep down in his heart, didn't appreciate the grind, the discipline," said Vince Lombardi. "I firmly believe that any man's finest hour—this greatest fulfillment to all he holds dear—is that moment when he has worked his heart out in a good cause and lies exhausted on the field of battle—victorious."

BECOME CHARACTER DRIVEN
INSTEAD OF EMOTION DRIVEN

"There are few ideal and leisurely settings for the disciplines of growth," according to Robert Thornton Henderson. Teddy Roosevelt said, "Ninety percent of the work is done in this country by people who don't feel well."

It is not doing the things we like to do, but doing the things we have to do that causes growth and makes us successful. John Luther said: "There's no such thing as a perfect job. In any position you'll find some duties which, if they aren't onerous immediately, eventually will be." Success depends not merely on how well you do the things you enjoy, but how conscientiously you perform those duties you don't.

List a few tasks that you must perform in your job that you find undesirable:

Task   **Benefit**

To the side, write the benefit of completing the task. If there isn't a benefit to the task, then you shouldn't do it. If there is a benefit to the task, then you should keep the results in mind while toiling away.

Successful people are willing to do things unsuccessful people will not do. My observation is that one thing that makes a difference is this issue of being character driven instead of emotion driven. This is the difference:

Character-Driven People	*Emotion-Driven People*
Do right, then feel good	Feel good, then do right
Are commitment driven	Are convenience driven
Make principle-based decisions	Make popularity based decisions
Allow action to control attitude	Allow attitude to control action
Believe it, then see it	See it, then believe it
Create momentum	Wait for momentum
Ask: "What are my responsibilities?"	Ask: "What are my rights?"
Continue when problems arise	Quit when problems arise
Are steady	Are moody
Are leaders	Are followers

APPLYING WHAT I'VE LEARNED

Good character is more to be praised than outstanding talent. Most talents are, to some extent, gifts. By contrast, good character is not given to us. We have to build it piece by piece—by thought, choice, courage, and determination. This will only be accomplished by maintaining a disciplined lifestyle.

How can you become more disciplined in your thoughts, choices, courage, and determination?

Thought:

Our thought life can strongly affect our actions. If any outside elements—such as other people or the media—are negatively affecting your thoughts, how can you avoid these things?

Choice:

There is always a choice in every situation. What steps can you take to ensure you are making right choices?

Courage and Determination:

Knowing that our actions make a difference can give us courage and keep us determined to reach a goal. List some ways that your actions can positively impact others.

SELF-DISCIPLINE
DISCUSSION QUESTIONS

1. This week you read about the peasant who was "king" of himself. What kinds of things commonly happen in the lives of people who are unable to govern themselves well?

2. In the second week you did a lot of work with priorities, including trying to set some for yourself. Review some of the decisions you made. How successful have you been at *keeping* your priorities in order?

3. Think about the overall priorities in your life. How would you rank the following in order of importance to you?
   A) Work
   B) Leisure
   C) Family
   D) Finances
   E) Ministry or volunteering
   F) Friendships and other relationships
   G) Personal time
   H) Other: _____

4. Everyone has to deal with calendar issues (even people who neglect to organize theirs). How do you approach your calendar when you work on it? Use the same list as in question 3. Which activities get put on your calendar first?

5. Does the way you approach your calendar match your stated priorities? If not, what kinds of changes do you need to make to put your priorities in order?

6. This week you read about the concept of pay now, play later. In what areas of your life have you paid a price up front in order to help you later? In what areas do you need to improve? Why?

7. One of the potential pitfalls of taking advice from other successful people is that they may give you recommendations based on their temperament, which may be different from your own. Describe yourself, including your temperament. What kinds of successful adjustments have you made to effectively work with the temperament God has given you? How could you improve?

8. What kinds of systems have you developed for yourself to be more efficient and self-disciplined?

9. Leaders are responsible for not only how they manage themselves, but how effectively they utilize all resources that have been entrusted to them, including people. How do you review and measure yourself in this area? Who holds you accountable for it?

Week 10

The Most Important Lesson of Leadership: *Staff Development*

INTRODUCTION

The growth and development of people is the highest calling of leadership. Week 7 emphasized the general development of people. This week will center on the development of a staff. But since it is impossible to go into depth on this important subject in one week, we will establish a foundation by focusing on the basics.

When I turned forty, I began to review my life. I made a list of all the things I was doing at that time. My list included:

- Senior pastor of a congregation of 3,500
- Oversight and development of thirteen pastors
- President of Injoy, Inc., a company that develops resource materials for thousands of people
- A national and international speaking schedule with over four hundred engagements annually
- Producing a monthly leadership tape for Injoy Life Club subscribers
- Writing a book every eighteen months
- Working on another education degree
- And most important—taking enough time for my wife, Margaret, and our two children, Elizabeth and Joel Porter

After writing out my list, my conclusion was twofold: I didn't have any more hours and therefore I couldn't work any harder; and my future growth in production would be determined by my ability to work through other people.

These two realities enabled me to search for and find the most important leadership lesson I've ever learned:

Those closest to the leader will determine the level of success for that leader.

Leaders who continue to grow personally and bring growth to their organizations will influence many and develop a successful team around them. The better the players, the better the leader. Few people are successful unless a lot of people want them to be.

Below is an illustration of what can happen to an organization when the key players slightly increase their potential.

$$3 \times 3 \times 3 \times 3 \times 3 = \underline{243} + 25\% \text{ increase individually}$$
$$4 \times 4 \times 4 \times 4 \times 4 = \underline{1024} + 400\% \text{ increase together}$$

A great leader develops a team of people who increase production. The result? The leader's influence and effectiveness begin to multiply (working through others) instead of adding (working by oneself). That "no man can sincerely try to help another without helping himself," is, according to Ralph Waldo Emerson, "one of the most beautiful compensations of this life."

All leaders have "war stories" of bad experiences in leading and developing staff. Perhaps this humorous illustration will help us laugh about our past experiences and allow us to get a second wind to begin building a winning team around us.

As nearly everyone knows, a leader has practically nothing to do except to decide what is to be done; tell somebody to do it; listen to reasons why it should not be done or why it should be done in a different way; follow up to see if the thing has been done; discover that it has not; inquire why; listen to excuses from the person who should have done it; follow up again to see if the thing has been done only to discover that it has been done incorrectly; point out how it should have been done; conclude that as long as it has been done, it may as well be left where it is; wonder if it is not time to get rid of a person who cannot do a thing right; reflect that the person probably has a spouse and a large family and any successor would be just as bad and maybe worse; consider how much simpler and better matters would be now if he had done it himself in the first place; reflect sadly that he could have done it right in twenty minutes and, as things turned out, he has had to spend two days to find out why it has taken three weeks for somebody else to do it wrong.[1]

In spite of all the problems that arise in the development of staff, two facts are certain. First, only as we develop a team do we continually succeed. A Chinese proverb says, "If you are planning for one year, grow rice. If you are planning for twenty years, grow trees. If you are planning for centuries, grow men." Second, only as we develop a team do we continually multiply.

This week, we will be looking at what makes up a winning team.

Winning teams . . .

- Have great leaders

- Pick good people

- Play to win

- Make other team members more successful

- Keep improving

As you work this week, begin to evaluate your team. How well do you function with them? How can you make improvements?

Day 1

Great Leaders

WINNING TEAMS HAVE GREAT LEADERS

There are two ways you can get others to do what you want: You can compel them to do it or you can persuade them. Compulsion is the method of slavery; persuasion is the method of free men, but persuading requires an understanding of what makes people tick and what motivates them—a knowledge of human nature. Great leaders possess that knowledge. If you understand what motivates people, you have at your command the most powerful tool for dealing with them.

During Week 1 you were asked to write out the needs and wants of your followers. Now, write out what motivates your followers—what makes them think, feel, and act as they do. (The two lists may be similar.)

Name   Motivation

People Management has been studying the personal histories of tens of thousands of people since 1961. The researchers found that, without exception, people repeat a pattern of behavior every time they accomplish something they think they do well and find deeply satisfying. They also found that excellent leaders underscore this behavior in the following ways:

Excellent leaders create the right environment. They believe in their team. This creates an environment for success. The best way to gain and hold the loyalty of your personnel is to show interest in and care for them by your words and actions.

Excellent leaders know basic human needs. Paul "Bear" Bryant, the legendary football coach at the University of Alabama, said there are five things winning team members need to know:

❑ What is expected from each one.

❑ That each will have an opportunity to perform.

❑ How each one is getting along.

❑ That guidance will be given where each needs it.

❑ That each will be rewarded according to his contribution.

For the five needs cited, place a check next to each item where you feel confident your team's needs are being met. For the items you are unable to check off, list a few ways you can better meet that need.

Excellent leaders keep control of the "Big 3." Any leader who wants to play an active role in all areas of the organization may be tempted to take on too many responsibilities. However, three areas are crucial to the leader's authority and success:

1. Finance: because the finance staff is a prime means of exercising executive control in any organization.

2. Personnel: because the selection of people will determine the direction of the organization.

3. Planning: because this area determines the future of the organization.

List who is currently in control of each area. If the person in control is someone other than yourself, write your role next to their name.

	Who's in control	My role as leader
Finance:	_____	_____
Personal:	_____	_____
Planning:	_____	_____

Excellent leaders avoid the "seven deadly sins."

1. Trying to be liked rather than respected.

2. Not asking team members for advice and help.

3. Thwarting personal talent by emphasizing rules rather than skills.

4. Not keeping criticism constructive.

5. Not developing a sense of responsibility in team members.

6. Treating everyone the same way.

7. Failing to keep people informed.

T. Boone Pickens said, "There are many ways to avoid mistakes, but the best way to sidestep the disasters is to be available. You don't have to make every decision, but you should always be accessible. If your people are smart, they will keep you informed, and if you're informed, you're a part of the decision. With that in place, it's easy for you to back your people and that eliminates second guessing."

APPLYING WHAT I'VE LEARNED

Sam Walton said, "Outstanding leaders go out of the way to boost the self-esteem of their personnel. If people believe in themselves, it's amazing what they can accomplish."

One of the "seven deadly sins" is treating everyone the same way. A good way to establish relationships with your followers is to recognize what makes them different.

List the names of the people on your team. Next to each name, write at least one positive thing that makes them unique.

Team Member　　　　　　　　**Unique Quality**

This week, take time to recognize at least three of the above people for their unique skill or quality. Let them know how they make a difference and contribute to the team.

Day 2

Good People

Today, we will look at methods of choosing the right team. Bobb Biehl says that 60 to 80 percent of the success of any company or organization is attributable to three factors:

1. A clear direction

2. The right team of players

3. Sound finances

That's why few things are as important as putting the right people in the right places. Getting the right people in the right places is crucial to the success of your organization. There are five principles for picking people that will help you get the best candidates on your team.

1. THE SMALLER THE ORGANIZATION, THE MORE IMPORTANT THE HIRING

Small organizations often make the mistake of thinking that they can get by with inferior staff members because they are small. The opposite is true. In a firm of one hundred employees, if one is inferior, the loss is only 1 percent. But if the organization has a payroll of two and one is inferior, the loss is 50 percent. However, on the bright side, it's much easier to pick one excellent person than a hundred.

2. KNOW WHAT KIND OF PERSON YOU NEED (PERSONAL REQUIREMENTS)

Listed below are the "Top 20" personal requirements I look for in a potential staff member:

1. Positive Attitude—the ability to see people and situations in a positive way.

2. High Energy Level—strength and stamina to work hard and not wear down.*

3. Personal Warmth—a manner that draws people to them.

4. Integrity—trustworthy, good, solid character; words and walk are consistent.

5. Responsible—always "comes through," no excuses; job delegated—job done.

6. Good Self-image—feels good about self, others, and life.

7. Mental Horsepower—ability to keep learning as the job expands.*

8. Leadership Ability—has high influence over others.

9. "Followership" Ability—willingness to submit, play team ball, and follow the leader.

10. Absence of Personal Problems—personal, family, and business life are in order.*

11. People Skills—the ability to draw people and develop them.

12. Sense of Humor—enjoys life, fails to take self too seriously.

13. Resilience—able to "bounce back" when problems arise.*

14. Track Record—has experience and success, hopefully in two or more situations.*

15. Great Desire—hungers for growth and personal development.

16. Self-discipline—willing to "pay the price" and handle success.

17. Creative—ability to see solutions and fix problems.

18. Flexibility—not afraid of change; fluid; flows as the organization grows.

19. Sees "Big Picture"—able to look beyond personal interest and see the total picture.

20. Intuitive—able to discern and sense a situation without tangible data.*

*These things probably cannot be taught. The others can be taught with a proper mentor, environment, and willingness by the staff member. Most of the qualities in the list can be evaluated with a couple of interviews and tests.

3. KNOW WHAT THE JOB REQUIRES

A job has certain characteristics that require specific skills and personality traits. These ten general questions will help a leader pick the right person.

Does the job require . . .

1. An up-front or a behind-the-scenes person?

2. A generalist or a specialist?

3. A producer or a maintainer?

4. A people person or a paper person?

5. A leader or a supporter?

6. A veteran or a rookie?

7. A creative thinker or an abstract one?

8. Constant supervision or a little supervision?

9. A team player or an individualist?

10. Short-term commitment or long-term commitment?

Often I am asked in leadership conferences, "How do you know which staff person to hire?" I always laugh and say, "You never know for sure," and my track record underscores that comment!

4. KNOW WHAT THE POTENTIAL STAFF MEMBER WANTS

People work harder, stay longer, and do better on the job when they like what they do. Realizing this truth, I always make sure the potential team player feels good about me as the leader, the other players on the team, and the vision and requirements of the team.

5. WHEN YOU CAN'T AFFORD TO HIRE THE BEST, HIRE THE YOUNG WHO ARE GOING TO BE THE BEST

Then:

Believe in them—that will encourage risk.

Show them—that will build respect.

Love them—that will strengthen relationships.

Know them—that will personalize development.

Teach them—that will enhance growth.

Trust them—that will develop loyalty.

Expand them—that will provide challenges.

Lift them—that will insure results.

APPLYING WHAT I'VE LEARNED

Theses are the guidelines I use for hiring staff. Make them specific to a position you will be hiring for in the near future.

Know what you need before you start looking for someone.

What are the job responsibilities? _____

What are the required skills or credentials? _____

Who would this person report to, and what is the supervisor's temperament?

(There are many tests your people can take to reveal their temperaments—if your

people have not already taken such tests, they need to.)_____

What type of person would work best with the supervisor?_____

Take time to search the field.

When do you need this person?

Call many references and check out the candidate's track record.

What type of references would help you to learn the most about this person's skills and character?

Have several interviews and include your close associates in some of the interviews and ask for their input.

Who should talk with this person before you hire them?

If possible, have a social interview where the candidate's spouse is included.

Who should be at this meeting?

If possible, have a trial run to see if the job and the candidate match.

How much time would it take to recognize this person's abilities?

Ask hard questions, such as, "Why did you leave?"; "What can you contribute?"; "Are you willing to pay the price?"

List other questions that should be asked:

Trust your instincts.

Day 3
Playing to Win

The difference between playing to win and playing not to lose is the difference between success and mediocrity. At every meeting, I remind my team to take risks, make tough decisions, live on the edge, and make a difference. People who play it safe continually miss opportunities and seldom make progress.

Are your workers giving their full effort and taking risks? How do you know?

A survey of workers across the United States revealed that nearly 85 percent of those interviewed said they could work harder on the job. More than half claimed they could double their effectiveness "if they wanted to."[1] Winning teams are seldom more talented than losing teams. But they are always more committed. They want to win. They pay the price and go after victory.

WINNING TEAMS MAKE THEIR TEAM MEMBERS MORE SUCCESSFUL

Robert W. Keidel said that trying to change individual and/or corporate behavior without addressing the larger organizational context is bound to disappoint. Sooner or later bureaucratic structures will consume even the most determined of collaborative processes. As Woody Allen once said, "The lion and the lamb may lie down together, but the lamb won't get much sleep."

What to do? Work on the lion as well as the lamb by designing teamwork into the organization. There are significant ways to engage in better team building.

Know the key to each player. Every individual has a personal agenda, the "real reason" he or she wants to be on the team. That personal agenda is the key to motivating each player. How well do you know the agendas of your key workers?

In the space provided, write down the names and agendas of several top workers.

Name   **Agenda**

Map out a team mission. Lay out the vision. Develop organizational mottos, names, symbols, and slogans. Doing this will encourage pride in team membership.

Define the role of each player. This will help avoid unnecessary rivalries by clearly identifying each person's role within the group. This will also avoid the "fairness" issue that is common with staffs. Each player will be appreciated for his or her contribution to the team.

Write down several key workers and specifically define their roles as you see them.

Name   **Role**

Create a group identity. Establish your group's worth by examining and promoting its history and values. Create memories together as a group.

Use liberal doses of "we" and "our." Team building involves getting the members to feel a sense of ownership in what they are doing as a group. When the group has done well, it is important to praise the entire effort without singling out individuals.

Communicate with everyone. Don't be a fact hog. Share information with everyone who is affected, not with just the key players. People are usually "down on" what they are not "up on." As a leader, you will know you have succeeded when the members of your team put the interests of the group over their own.

APPLYING WHAT I'VE LEARNED

These areas of team building are significant. They make each person stronger through their participation on the team.

Of the six areas of team building, where do you most need to improve?

What are some steps you can take to grow in this area?

Day 4

Improvement

WINNING TEAMS KEEP IMPROVING

Why is it that a professional football, basketball, or baseball team seldom repeats as the world champion in consecutive years? Mainly it's because of the temptation to keep all the players, practices, and strategies the same as the previous year. Too many think that if they "stay put" they can stay on top. That's not true. Either the current players must keep growing and improving, or potentially better ones must be brought into the organization.

CONTINUED SUCCESS IS A RESULT
OF CONTINUED IMPROVEMENT

The first objective of the leader is to develop people, not to dismiss them. Studies have shown that day-to-day coaching, rather than comprehensive annual appraisals, is most effective for improving performance. This coaching process has two crucial components: setting specific objectives and holding frequent progress reviews.

Objectives. Objectives should specify end results, the exact extent of achievement the manager expects. They should also be tied to a timetable. How many objectives should the employee be given? In our experience, a few are better than too many. If the subordinate is overloaded, expecting all the objectives to be accomplished is unreasonable. Remember, the objectives are the primary measuring stick.

For one of the member of your team, list the objectives you have given them or need to give them for a particular project. Also list the deadline for each task.

Team member: _____

Objective 1:

    Completed by:_____

Objective 2:

    Completed by:_____

Objective 3:

    Completed by:_____

Objective 4:

    Completed by:_____

Objective 5:

    Completed by:_____

End Results. By *end results*, we mean what should be observably different as a result of the subordinate's performance on the job. All too often employees expect to be evaluated on the basis of how much effort they are putting into the job, rather than what they are accomplishing. This is especially true of weak performers. It is critical that the manager make clear that certain outcomes are expected and the subordinate will be held accountable for them. The manager should make every effort to set mutually acceptable goals.

What should the end result be for the objectives?

Progress Reports/Reviews. Frequent progress reviews accomplish three things. First, they serve as a continual reminder that reaching the objectives is important to the person's career. Second, reviews give the manager a chance to recognize positive movement toward objectives. Third, if progress is not forthcoming, the manager can listen to the reasons for lack of performance and attempt to get the subordinate on track. The review becomes a problem-solving session.

Whether or not the employee makes progress, holding reviews permits the manager or boss to remain in control of the process.[2] If you have more than three people reporting to you right now, chances are that you are unhappy with at least one of them. The situation usually has one or more of these elements:

- The person is not doing a top-notch job, but not a terrible one either; so you keep him or her around.

- Finding someone else who can do the job means interviewing, hiring (taking a risk), and then training the new person. You do not have time for that either.

- The person definitely is not doing the job, but you like him or her (or more likely you feel sorry for him or her).

- You don't quite have all the documentation you need to fire this person. Your last review was too flowery and you have not really said how unhappy you are with the individual's work.

The result? Nothing happens. Remember, it isn't the people you fire who make your life miserable; it's the ones you don't. If you have serious doubts about a staff member and have worked with him or her without success, it is better to have that person working somewhere else.

If you currently have a team member who you would like to remove from your team, why haven't you done so yet?

Keep in mind that you and the person who needs to be dismissed are not the only two people in the equation.

- The situation is well known to other workers in the organization. No one can keep below-par performance a secret.

- Your failure to fire will have a detrimental effect on your career. As a leader, your first and greatest responsibility is to the organization and its highest good. Whenever a person's leadership position puts the personal agenda of himself or herself ahead of the organization, that leader is a liability.

- The morale of the other employees suffers because you keep the below-par performer on the payroll while everyone else is pulling more than enough weight.

How can dismissing a person be handled correctly? Bobb Biehl says the essence of doing it right is in maintaining this perspective: "When you appropriately fire a person from a position in which he is failing, you are actually releasing him from that failure—and freeing him to seek a position in which he can find success. With a proper release, it's even possible to instill in the person the excitement that comes from anticipating a new venture."

APPLYING WHAT I'VE LEARNED

In order to make more routine and effective evaluations, you may want to develop a calendar and journal for your progress reports. Do these evaluations often and regularly. Use the following example to keep routine records of your employee's evaluations:

Name	Evaluation Date	Comments
_____	_____	_____
	_____	_____
		_____
_____	_____	_____
	_____	_____
		_____

Day 5

The Strengths of a Leader

As we end this study, let's stop to consider your strengths as a leader. This evaluation will allow you to review the areas of importance to a leader, while reinforcing the areas you need to emphasize in your personal development. Simply circle the number that corresponds with how you see your ability right now.

1	2	3	4	5
Mastered	Strong	Satisfactory	Needs Growth	Difficult

COMMON STRENGTHS
OUTSTANDING LEADERS SHARE

Dreaming: 1 2 3 4 5
Never let go of a dream until you're ready to wake up and make it happen.
In working with leaders, I have often asked myself, "Does the man make the dream, or does the dream make the man?" My conclusion: Both are equally true.

Goal Setting: 1 2 3 4 5
A goal is a dream with a deadline.
If you don't know what you want and where you are going, you will get next to nothing and end up nowhere.

Influencing: 1 2 3 4 5
The very essence of all power to influence lies in getting the other person to participate. People do not care how much you know until they know how much you care.

Personal Organization: 1 2 3 4 5
"Organizing is something you do before you do something, so that when you do it, it's not all mixed up."— Christopher Robin in *Winnie the Pooh*

Prioritizing: 1 2 3 4 5
"He is a wise man who wastes no energy on pursuits for which he is not fitted; and he is wiser still who, from the things he can do well, chooses and resolutely follows the best."—William Gladstone

Problem Solving: 1 2 3 4 5
"The majority see the obstacles; the few see the objectives; history records the successes of the latter, while oblivion is the reward of the former."—Alfred Armand Montapert

Risk Taking: 1 2 3 4 5
Risks are to be evaluated not in terms of success, but in terms of the value of the goal.

Decision Making: 1 2 3 4 5
Your decisions will always be better if you do what is right for the organization rather than what is right for yourself.

Creativity: 1 2 3 4 5
There is always a better way . . . your challenge is to find it.
"Man's mind, once stretched by a new idea, never regains its original dimensions."
—Oliver Wendell Holmes

Hiring/Firing: 1 2 3 4 5
"There are only three rules of sound administration: pick good [people], tell them not to cut corners, and back them to the limit."—Adlai E. Stevenson

Evaluation: 1 2 3 4 5
People who reach their potential spend more time asking, "What am I doing well?" rather than "What am I doing wrong?"

The person who knows *how* will always have a job; but the person who knows *why* will always be the boss.

WHAT POTENTIAL LEVEL ARE YOU ON?

You always want to maximize your greatest potential. There are three levels of potential:

1. I maximize my potential (I pour my energy into myself).

2. I maximize the potential of others (I pour my energy into key people).

3. They maximize my potential (they pour their energy into me).

- Producers excel only at level 1.

- Leaders excel at levels 1 and 2.

- Fortunate leaders excel at levels 1 and 2 and experience level 3.

- If you are strong in or have mastered four areas, you are on level 1.

- If you are strong in or have mastered eight areas, you are on level 2.

- If you are strong in or have mastered every area, you are on level 3, and that means you have a strong support team that has allowed you to grow beyond yourself.

My hope is that you work hard at arriving at level 3. You have the opportunity to be a great leader!

STAFF DEVELOPMENT
DISCUSSION QUESTIONS

1. Why is the growth and development of people called the highest calling of leadership?

2. To increase effectiveness, leaders really have only three options. In which of the three areas listed below do you still have room for improvement?
   A) Working harder (a matter of vision, self-discipline, attitude, or integrity)
   B) Working smarter (a matter of priorities or problem solving)
   C) Working through others (a matter of influence, people skills, staff development, or the ability to effect change)

3. What kind of priority do you give the development of others as leaders? Specifically, what have you done in the past month to develop some of the individuals you lead?

4. For an organization to be successful, it must win in three areas. Which of the three is your strength? Why?
   A) Finances
   B) Personnel
   C) Planning

5. No leader can excel in every area, yet no area can afford to be neglected. One of the keys to leading effectively is to hire and develop people in your areas of weakness. Have you surrounded yourself with people who will ensure success in the two areas where you are weaker? If not, why not. If you have, are you empowering them and setting them up to succeed?

6. Sometimes as you hire people, you must choose between a proven performer and a rookie with potential. Which do you tend to choose? Why?

7. This week you read about knowing the "key" to a person's life. What have you done in the past to discover the key in the people you lead?

8. Why is turning that "key" both a privilege and a serious responsibility?

9. What does it mean to take someone you lead to the next level? Have you done this with someone before? Describe the process and the outcome.

10. What are you doing today that could be done by leaders you helped to develop? How will you go about making that happen?

Notes

Introduction

1. John W. Gardner, "The Nature of Leadership," Leadership Papers #1, Independent Sector, January 1986.

2. Richard Kerr for United Technologies Corp., *Bits and Pieces*, March 1990.

Week 1

1. James C. Georges, ParTraining Corp., Tucker, GA, interviewed in *Executive Communications*, January 1987.

2. J. R. Miller, *The Building of Character* (New Jersey: AMG Publishers, 1975).

3. Warren Bennis and Burt Nanus, *Leaders* (New York: Harper & Row, 1985), 222.

4. Robert Dilenschneider, *Power and Influence: Mastering the Art of Persuasion* (New York: Prentice Hall, 1990).

Week 3

1. Dwight D. Eisenhower, *Great Quotes from Great Leaders*, ed. Peggy Anderson (Lombard: Great Quotations, 1989).

2. Peter Drucker, *Management, Tasks, Responsibilities and Practices* (New York: Harper & Row, 1974).

3. *Newsweek*, 24 August 1987, 11.

4. Joseph Bailey, "Clues for Success in the President's Job," *Harvard Business Review*, 1983.

5. James Kouzes and Barry Posner, *The Leadership Challenge* (San Francisco: Jossey-Bass, 1987).

Week 4

1. Quoted in Paul Wharton, *Stories and Parables for Preachers and Teachers* (Mahwah: Paulist, 1986).

2. Howard Hendricks, *Teaching to Change Lives* (Portland: Multnomah, 1987), 32.

Week 5

1. F. F. Fournies, *Coaching for Improved Work Performance* (New York: Van Nostrand Reinhold, 1978).

2. Taken from a quotation by MacDonald in *Leaves of Gold*, A. C. Remley (Williamsport: Coslett Publishing, 1948).

3. Adapted from G. W. Target, "The Window," in the *Window and Other Essays* (Mountain View: Pacific Press Publishing Association, 1973), 5–7.

4. Bobb Biehl, *Increasing Your Leadership Confidence* (Sister: Questar Publishers, 1989).

5. John K. Clemens, *Hartwick Humanities in Management Report* (Oneonta: Hartwick Institute, 1989).

Week 6

1. Charles Swindoll, *Improving Your Serve* (Waco: Word, 1981).

2. Nell Mohney, "Beliefs Can Influence Attitudes," *Kingsport Times News*, 25 July 1986, 4B.

3. Norman Vincent Peale, *Power of the Plus Factor* (New York: Fawcett, 1988).

4. Anonymous, "Attitude," *Bartlett's Familiar Quotations*, ed. Emily Morison Beck (Boston: Little Brown, 1980).

5. Viktor Frankl, "Youth in Search of Meaning," *Moral Development Foundations*, ed. Donald M. Joy (Nashville: Abingdon, 1983).

6. C. S. Lewis, *Mere Christianity* (New York: Macmillan, 1952), 86.

Week 7

1. Stephen Ash, "The Career Doctor," cited in Michigan Department of Social Services, *No-Name Newsletter*, fall 1986.

Week 8

1. Robert K. Greenleaf, *The Servant as Leader* (Mahwah: Paulist, 1977).

2. Biehl, *Increasing Your Leadership Confidence*.

3. Harry C. McKown, *A Boy Grows Up* (New York: McGraw-Hill, 1985).

4. George S. Patton, *Great Quotes from Great Leaders*.

5. Ralph Waldo Emerson, *Bartlett's Familiar Quotations*.

6. Roger von Oech, *A Kick in the Seat of the Pants* (San Francisco: HarperCollins, 1986).

Week 9

1. Harry S. Truman, *Great Quotes from Great Leaders*.

2. Edwin Markham, *Great Quotes from Great Leaders*.

3. Edward Everett Hale, *Bartlett's Familiar Quotations*.

Week 10

1. Richard Huseman and John Hatfield, *Managing the Equity Factor* (New York: Houghton Mifflin, 1989).

2. William J. Morin and Lyle Yorks, *Dismissal* (San Diego: Harcourt Brace Jovanovich, 1990).

About the Author

John C. Maxwell, known as America's expert on leadership, speaks in person to hundreds of thousands of people each year. He has communicated his leadership principles to Fortune 500 companies, the United States Military Academy at West Point, and sports organizations such as the NCAA, the NBA, and the NFL.

Maxwell is the founder of several organizations, including Maximum Impact, dedicated to helping people reach their leadership potential. He is the author of more than thirty books, including *Developing the Leader Within You, Your Road Map for Success,* and *The 21 Irrefutable Laws of Leadership,* which has sold more than one million copies.

ORGANIZATIONAL PROFILE

maximumimpact™

www.maximumimpact.com

MAXIMUM IMPACT™ HAS 5 CHANNELS OF CUSTOMER ENGAGEMENT

Corporate Training

Customized Training Solutions for you and your team. We offer open-enrollment, on-location, and train-the-trainer formats. For more details go to: **www.maximumimpact.com/training**

Events

Powerful conferences with incredible speaker line-ups. Past speakers have included: Rudy Giuliani, Ken Blanchard, Jack Welch, Marcus Buckingham, Bobby Bowden, and more! For more details go to: **www.maximumimpact.com/conferences**

Subscriptions

Leadership develops daily, not in a day. Leadership disciplines and habits require constant attention. Our subscription-based monthly mentoring delivers training to you in the form of an audio CD. Go to: **www.maximumimpact.com/monthlyaudio**

Resources

Thousands of topical resources, books, training kits (DVD), audio CDs, web resources, and more. Just what you need to grow as a business and sales leader or as a strong team. For more details go to: **www.maximumimpact.com/resources**

Speakers

Keynote, half-day, and full-day presentations by America's best-known authorities tailored to your organization's needs. For more details go to: **www.maximumimpact.com/speakers**

 mi ONLINE

Visit us at **www.maximumimpact.com** to learn more about how your organization can benefit from our all-in-one solutions.

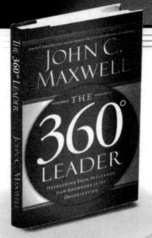

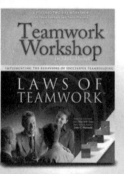

Books by Dr. John C. Maxwell can teach you how to be a REAL success

RELATIONSHIPS

Be a People Person
(Victor Books)

Becoming a Person of Influence
(Nelson Business)

The Power of Influence
(Honor Books)

**The Power of Partnership
in the Church**
(J. Countryman)

Relationships 101
(Nelson Business)

The Treasure of a Friend
(J. Countryman)

Winning with People
(Nelson Business)

25 Ways to Win with People
(Nelson Business)

ATTITUDE

Be All You Can Be
(Victor Books)

Failing Forward
(Nelson Business)

The Power of Thinking
(Honor Books)

Living at the Next Level
(Nelson Business)

Think on These Things
(Beacon Hill)

The Winning Attitude
(Nelson Business)

Your Bridge to a Better Future
(Nelson Business)

The Power of Attitude
(Honor Books)

EQUIPPING

Developing the Leaders
Around You
(Nelson Business)

Equipping 101
(Nelson Business)

Partners in Prayer
(Nelson Business)

Your Road Map for Success
(Nelson Business)

Your Road Map
for Success Workbook
(Nelson Business)

Success One Day at a Time
(J. Countryman)

The 17 Indisputable
Laws of Teamwork
(Nelson Business)

The 17 Essential Qualities
of a Team Player
(Nelson Business)

LEADERSHIP

The 21 Indispensable
Qualities of a Leader
(Nelson Business)

The 21 Irrefutable
Laws of Leadership
(Nelson Business)

The 21 Most Powerful Minutes
in a Leader's Day
(Nelson Business)

Developing the Leader
Within You Workbook
(Nelson Business)

Developing the Leader Within You
(Nelson Business)

The Power of Leadership
(Honor Books)

The Right to Lead
(J. Countryman)

 **Additional Notes**